Understanding, Managing & Redeeming Church Conflict

by Leroy Goertzen, D.Min.

Understanding, Managing & Redeeming Church Conflict
Copyright © 2012 Leroy Goertzen, D.Min.

You can write to the author at lgoertzen@corban.edu.

Additional copies of this book are available for sale online at
www.CreateSpace.com
www.BooksaMillion.com
www.BarnesandNoble.com
www.Amazon.com

Contents

Why This Book?

This book has put up quite the fight. It started as a chapter in my doctoral dissertation examining literature pertinent to the subject of church conflict. Instead of staying put, though, it took on a life of its own beyond the dissertation itself. Finally, after several requests, I've agreed to publish it as a stand-alone volume for use by any and all within the Church.

I'm glad to report a significant body of literature regarding church conflict expounds proven principles we can use. In particular, this book will review church conflict literature that focuses on 1) introductory concepts to church conflict, 2) the inevitability of church conflict, and 3) the nature of church conflict, 4) the management of church conflict, and 5) the redemption of church conflict.

Like any book, this has many limitations. For one, it is an historic document, sharing the same birth year as my dissertation. For another, it's not the last word on church conflict. Still, the biblical, theological, and psychological principles presented in this book are timeless. They're as applicable today as ever.

If this book proves useful to you, and your church, please let me know. You can reach me via email at lgoertzen@corban.edu.

An Introduction to
Church Conflict Management

Church conflict literature covers a broad spectrum of issues. Some literature provides a preliminary perspective to church conflict as part of a more complex problem.

The objective of most of the literature is to offer an approach to managing conflict; but in doing so, it assumes a significant knowledge regarding the nature of church conflict itself.

Thus, as part of this foundational material, literature will be examined that contributes to our understanding of Church conflict's extent and definition.

The Extent of Church Conflict

Conflict management becomes increasingly important when one understands how prevalent significant conflict is and why the church is particularly vulnerable.

The Church is Experiencing Significant Conflict

The anecdotal material of the literature testifies that church conflict is prominent. Robert Clinton observes: "Leaders are constantly dealing with conflict...most leaders spend the majority of their time and energy dealing with conflict."[1] H.B. London's findings support Clinton's remark; 75% of pastors experience a significant stress-related crisis monthly in their ministry.[2]

A 1996 Leadership survey discovered, however, that pastors ranked handling church conflict fifth in a short list of necessary pastoral skills.[3] Church members have noticed. Speed Leas reports that 46 percent of conflict involves the pastor's interpersonal competence.[4]

A Leadership 2004 survey reports that 38 percent of pastors have left a pastoral position due to conflict, a likely occurrence since 77 percent of congregants view the pastor as the center of most problems.[5] But problems don't stay with the pastor as Thom Rainer's survey indicates; nearly 72 percent of members left a church due to interpersonal

---

[1] Robert J. Clinton, *The Making of a Leader* (Colorado Springs, CO: Nav Press, 1988), 162.

[2] H. B. London and Neil Wiseman, *Pastors at Risk* (Wheaton, IL: Victor Books, 1993), 22.

[3] David L. Goetz, "Forced Out," *Leadership* 17:1 (Winter 1996): 48.

[4] Speed B. Leas, "Inside Church Fights: An Interview with Speed Leas," *Leadership* 10:1 (Winter 1989): 15.

[5] Eric Reed, "Leadership Surveys Church Conflict," *Leadership* 25:4 (Fall 2004): 25.

conflict (28 percent) and wounded feelings (44 percent).[6]

Such responses make Jerrien Gunnink's study believable; continuously in the US alone, there are at least 30,000 Protestant churches in serious conflict,[7] a situation that leads to the division of nearly 15,000 churches annually.[8] As Lyndel Moe correctly tabulates, "roughly eight percent of the churches have serious internal conflict at any given time, and approximately half of these will split each year."[9]

One can take seriously, then, the warning of Dr. Roy Roberts, who Susek quotes as saying, "No church is more than twenty-four hours away from a major conflict breaking out."[10] Such statistics, alarming as they are, indicate the need for conflict management, but also simply reflect the obvious;

---

[6] Thom S. Rainer, *High Expectations* (Nashville, TN: Broadman & Holman Publishers, 1999), 160.

[7] Gene Edwards and Tom Brandon, *Preventing a Church Split* (Scarborough, ME: Christian Books, 1987), 11.

[8] Ibid., 8.

[9] Lyndel John Moe, "A Comparison of Two Analytical Models for Understanding Local Church Conflict" (D. Miss. diss., Biola University, 1999), 2.

[10] Ron Susek, *Firestorm* (Grand Rapids, MI: Baker Books, 1999), 12.

the Church in general and Christians in particular are not immune to conflict: "it affects every dimension of our lives."[11]

The Church Is Vulnerable to Conflict

Within sociological circles, there appears a troubling belief; that churches are more vulnerable to intense conflict and difficult behavior than other institutions. Peter Steinke quotes Edwin Freidman as saying:

> Actually religious institutions are the worst offenders at encouraging immaturity and irresponsibility. In church after church, some member is passively-aggressively holding the whole system hostage, and no one wants to fire him or force her to leave because it wouldn't be "the Christian thing to do."[12]

It is this reality that Paul Stevens and Phil Collins have in mind in their evaluation: "Many emotionally and spiritually weak people . . . dominate the church."[13]

Clinical psychologist and pastor, Kenneth Haugk agrees, "For too long, congregations have been places where antagonists can operate with success. Their behavior is not

---

[11] Donald C. Palmer, *Managing Conflict Creatively* (Pasadena, CA: William Carey Library, 1990), 5.

[12] Peter Steinke, *How Your Church Family Works* (Bethesda, MD: Alban Institute, 1993), 59.

[13] Kenneth Alan Moe, *The Pastor's Survival Manual* (Bethesda, MD: Alban Institute, 1995), 51.

as successful in many other areas of life because … it is simply not tolerated."[14]

Statements such as this are not intended to suggest that every church is relationally dysfunctional and therefore necessarily conflicted. They do, however, propose that the very nature of the church as an organization and as a body politic makes it more predisposed than many other agencies to the influence and control of emotionally disturbed and mentally incompetent people and their conflictive behaviors. The anecdotal material here is overwhelming, coming in particular from those authors who also serve as church conflict consultants.[15]

Arthur Boers believes there are at least thirteen factors within the church's organizational system that tend to make it more vulnerable to conflict: 1) "Accomplices" of conflict—difficult behavior is often permitted, if not enabled by conflict-avoiding parishioners, 2) passive responders—difficult behavior is often placated or appeased out of naïveté or the desire for peace, 3) rituals and social constraints—the inability to set appropriate boundaries for those who are

---

[14] Kenneth C. Haugk, *Antagonists in the Church* (Minneapolis, MN: Augsburg Publishing House, 1988), 39.

[15] Several of the authors/church conflict consultants and their books would include: Speed Leas, *Moving Your Church through Conflict*; Ken Sande, *The Peacemaker*; Ron Susek, *Firestorm*; and Jim Van Yperen, *Making Peace*.

"persistent, intrusive, and aggressive," 4) a further bind: the price of togetherness—church members tolerate difficult behavior as the price to be paid for fellowship, 5) the interior stakes—church members' deep investment in their faith is coupled to their self-concept making matters of belief and practice deeply personal, 6) the eternal stakes of church conflict—disputes are often framed around the ultimate dichotomy; heaven and hell, 7) religious language can preclude healthy discernment—terminology is often spiritually loaded, justifying "absurd behavior," 8) the pressures of high goals—churches are often characterized by impossible expectations, which when unmet, lead to disillusion and anger, 9) challenging the status quo—the Gospel's call for "social and personal transformation" "raises unsettling questions" about many of life's assumed values and beliefs, 10) volunteer organizations and inappropriate uses of power—because volunteers are esteemed for their self-sacrifice, their behavior is often overlooked and accountability is minimized, 11) the effect of excluding some from power—neglected parishioners and those alienated from position and power will become dissatisfied, 12) the hazards of small organizations—small churches are inevitably effected by every conflict while difficult behavior must be tolerated to maintain critical mass, 13) other contributors to difficult behavior—"pastoral ghosts": the memories and legacy of a previous long-term or especially influential pastor.[16]

This substantial list represents the general insight of the literature as to why the church seems particularly vulnerable to conflict.

What is essential to see in these factors of vulnerability is their central theme—issues that are "systems" oriented. Cosgrove and Hatfield, utilizing a Family Systems theory of conflict management, note that,

> ...behind the official system of the local church, its offices, boards, committees, etc., there is another system, a family-like system which powerfully determines the way the church members relate to one another, do business together, and are for one another, and fight with one another. [17]

Not all the writers in church conflict management would necessarily agree with the entire approach of Family Systems Theory, but that the church is entirely unique as an institution made up of individuals and families is unquestioned.

The implication is that the church is not only required to deal with the struggles that are ordinary to any institution

---

[16] Paul Boers, *Never Call Them Jerks* (Bethesda, MD: Alban Institute, 1999), 19-24.

[17] Charles H. Cosgrove and Dennis D. Hatfield, *Church Conflict: The Hidden Systems Behind the Fights* (Nashville, TN: Abingdon Press, 1994), 5.

or organization, but that its situation is complicated by the fact that, more than any other institution, it must also deal with the relational dynamics of a family system. This provides the ultimate explanation as to why the church is so vulnerable to conflict.

In a powerful way, the statistics in the previous section demonstrate that the church's vulnerability to conflict is real and should be taken seriously in any management theory.

The Basic Components of "Church Conflict"

The successful management of church conflict requires knowledge of basic conflict theory. Foundational, then, is the development of a definition of conflict and an understanding of the elements that make up conflict and their relationship to one another.

The Definition of "Church Conflict"

A discussion of conflict management requires that conflict be defined. The first works on church conflict lack clarity in defining conflict.[18] An early definition is that of Ross Stagner: "a situation in which two or more human beings desire goals which they perceive as being attainable

---

[18] Moe, "A Comparison of Two Analytical Models for Understanding Local Church Conflict", 15.

by one or the other but not by both" (*The Dimensions of Human Conflict*, 136).[19]

Larry McSwain adapted this concept for his own definition: "Conflict describes those experiences of individuals and groups trying to achieve goals which are either incompatible or appear to be so."[20]

Leas and Kittlaus, whose book, *Church Fights*, is considered the seminal work in the field, offered this mechanistic definition in 1973: "Conflict happens when two pieces of matter try to occupy the same space at the same time."[21] This definition is based on the Latin word for "conflict," *fligere*, meaning "to strike together."[22]

---

[19] Speed B. Leas and Paul Kittlaus, *Church Fights: Managing Conflict in the Local Church* (Philadelphia: Westminster Press, 1973), 28-29.

[20] Larry L. McSwain and William C. Treadwell, Jr., *Conflict Ministry in the Church* (Nashville, TN: Broadman Press, 1981), 25.

[21] Leas and Kittlaus, *Church Fights: Managing Conflict in the Local Church*, 28.

[22] Ibid.

Douglas Lewis adapts this definition; conflict is "two or more objects trying to occupy the same space at the same time."[23]

An earlier definition from outside church circles, helped frame more recent attempts. Lewis Coser defines conflict as "a struggle over values and claims to scarce status, power and resources in which the aims of the opponents are to neutralize, injure or eliminate their rivals" (*The Functions of Social Conflict*, 8).[24] Coser includes competition over scarce products and negative intent.

Similarly, Joseph Himes defines conflict as the "purposeful struggles between collective actors who use social power to defeat or remove opponents and to gain status, power, resources and other scarce values."[25] Himes stresses the purpose of the conflict—the gaining of scarce commodities.

Coser and Himes have been followed closely by numerous church conflict writers. Examples include Kreider

---

[23] G. Douglass Lewis, *Resolving Church Conflicts: A Case Study Approach for Local Congregations* (San Francisco: Harper and Row, 1981), 5.

[24] Kenneth O. Gangel and Samuel L. Canine, *Communication and Conflict Management in Churches and Christian Organizations* (Nashville, TN: Broadman Press, 1992), 131.

[25] J. S. Himes, *Conflict and Conflict Management* (Athens, GA: University of Georgia Press, 1980), 14.

and Goossen who define conflict as "A natural part of human experience in which two or more parties believe they have incompatible objectives (e.g., power or limited resources) leading them to try to hurt, subdue, or neutralize the other party."[26] Halverstadt states that "Conflicts are power struggles over differences: differing information or differing belief; differing interests, desires, or values; different abilities to secure needed resources."[27] Jay Hall defines conflict as "circumstances, both emotional and substantive, which can be brought about by differences between parties who are, for whatever reason, in contact with one another."[28]

Family Systems theory advocate, Dennis Cosgrove, recognizes the difficulty in defining conflict: "It is impossible to give a simple definition of conflict, except to say that it is the expression (in words and actions) of disharmony between different opinions and desires present in all human systems."[29] One can notice the attempt to understand

[26] Robert S. Kreider and Rachel Waltner Goossen, *When Good People Quarrel: Studies in Conflict Resolution* (Scottdale, PA: Herald Press, 1989), 177.

[27] Hugh F. Halverstadt, *Managing Church Conflict* (Louisville, KY: Westminster/John Knox Press, 1991), 4.

[28] Jay Hall, *Conflict Management Survey* (Woodlands, TX: Teleometrics International, Inc., 1996), inside cover page.

[29] Cosgrove and Hatfield, 19-20.

conflict, not so much as interpersonal or intrapersonal, but communal.

From the Reconciliation approach to conflict, Ken Sande defines conflict as "a difference in opinion or purpose that frustrates someone's goals or desires."[30] The focus on "desires" is undoubtedly an attempt to capture the essence of James 4:1-2 where "desires" are seen as the dynamic source of conflict. Thus, Van Yperen states, "Conflict is the result of unwarranted and unfulfilled desire."[31]

Not all literature fits these categories. Newton Maloney, for example, believes that "much thinking about conflict suffers from a lack of clarity." This lack of clarity pertains to what he sees as a sharp distinction between "conflict" and "problems."[32] He understands problems to be the "differences of opinions about the ways, means or ends of dealing with real-life issues" while conflict is the "desperate

---

[30] Ken Sande, *The Peacemaker: A Biblical Guide to Resolving Personal Conflict*, 3rd ed. (Grand Rapids, MI: Baker Books, 2004), 13.

[31] Jim Van Yperen, *Making Peace* (Chicago: Moody Press, 2002), 94.

[32] H. Newton Malony, *Win-Win Relationships: 9 Strategies for Settling Personal Conflict without Waging War* (Nashville, TN: Broadman & Holman Publishers, 1995), x.

feelings of threats to one's self esteem that can lead to drastic acts of self-defense."[33]

It is apparent that problems, then, deal with ideas and are situational while conflicts involve feelings and are personal. With that distinction in mind, he defines conflict as "a desperate state of mind in which people feel their self-esteem is so endangered that something desperate must be done to restore it."[34]

The distinction here goes beyond conflicts and problems; it is between intrapersonal and interpersonal conflict. Most of the literature sees this distinction as "kinds" of conflict rather than part of conflict's definition.

The Dimensions of Church Conflict

All definitions of conflict admittedly require explanation and illustration since they are more an attempt to describe results than essence. This has led some writers as McSwain and Treadwell to simply state, "What should be analyzed are the consequences of conflict, not the conflict itself."[35] Though this appears to be a fundamentally flawed and limiting approach, it does point to the need to describe

---

[33] Ibid., xi.

[34] H. Newton Malony, *When Getting Along Seems Impossible* (Old Tappan, NJ: Fleming H. Revell Co., 1989), 18.

[35] McSwain and Treadwell, 118.

the basic elements of conflict, those defining characteristics that describe the essential substance of conflict's activity.

The literature notes that common to most definitions of conflict are several key elements or dimensions. Gangel and Canine, whose conflict management perspective reflects communication theory and administrative processes, offers one of the more comprehensive lists; 1) Interdependency—the connection of the participants, 2) interactive struggle—the feeling of tension from an opponent seeking to move us in an unwanted direction, 3) incompatible goals—the opponent plans to end up at a different location, 4) perceived interference—the opponent appears to be hindering or seeking to thwart our efforts, and 5) interface of opposition and cooperation—though the conflicted parties are fighting, they are also likely to share a common membership to a social group within which the conflict transpires.[36]

These five elements are better appreciated against the backdrop of Lewis Coser's or Jay Hall's definition of conflict. Jay Hall has dissected his definition into two dimensions; 1) personal relevance, i.e., goals and how much we value them, and 2) context, the relationships in which conflict occurs and how much we value them. Hall would also argue, as does Gangel, that conflict requires interdependency. For Hall, "personal relevance" measures the strength of an individual's

---

[36] Gangel and Canine, 131-132.

commitment to his goals when they are mutually exclusive, and, when commonly desired commodities are in short supply.[37] Lewis offers this simplified version of conflict's dimensions: 1) resources—what people are competing for, and 2) intention—the goals of each party.[38] These elements are easily recognized in the previous lists, but what is missing is the relational component and the degree to which the parties in conflict value both the goals pursued and the relationships involved.

In *Creative Conflict in Religious Education and Church Administration*, Bossart states that there are at least three elements present in every church conflict: "ineffective communication, threatened identity, and intransigence."[39] These three elements are also recognizable in Gangel and Canine's list, but shift the angle of perception; namely, how conflict is experienced interpersonally and intrapersonally.

It seems that most writers have missed an important element—the use of power—a factor given greater consideration in secular literature. In his dissertation, Lyndel Moe demonstrates the validity of the Power Model for use in

---

[37] Hall, 14.

[38] Lewis, 5.

[39] Donald E. Bossart, *Creative Conflict in Religious Education and Church Administration* (Birmingham, AL: Religious Education Press, 1980), 230.

church conflict settings.[40] He has defined "social power" as "using an asset to move people toward a desired goal."[41] This definition includes several elements of its own: 1) power—the force or influence being exerted by the social actors to coerce, compensate, or condition the opposition, 2) assets—the instruments or commodities being used to move or overpower the opposing party, 3) goals—the purpose/s of the social actors in the conflict, and 4) point of conflict—the area or issue about which the conflict is focused.[42] The resemblances to Gangel and Canine's classification of elements are striking, but include the essential perspective of power, a valuable insight considering its emphasis in the teachings of Jesus and the Apostles.

Additionally, Speed Leas would contend that his model of conflict management would necessitate the consideration of the meaning and implications of the language used to communicate to the opposing party.[43] This becomes a means of determining conflict's level of intensity and helps to determine management's strategy.

---

[40] Moe, "A Comparison of Two Analytical Models for Understanding Local Church Conflict", 31-66.

[41] Ibid., 65.

[42] Ibid., 66.

[43] Speed B. Leas, *Moving Your Church through Conflict* (Washington, D.C: Alban Institute, 1985), 19.

The Need for Church
Conflict Management

It seems apparent that the presence of conflict requires management. But the statistics in the first section demonstrate this may not be obvious. Two factors help explain at a deeper level why church conflict management is necessary; the fact that conflict is inevitable and that the Scriptures exhort the Body of Christ to live in unity.

The Inevitability of Church Conflict

The extent of conflict in the church brings to bear the question of its inevitability. Is it an aberration to be eliminated or is it as Vale and Hughes suggest, "a fact of life" that "we can't avoid" but "can only learn from"?[44] Most writers recognize the inevitability of conflict in that it is a normal and necessary part of life. Kreider and Goossen maintain that "the starting point for effectiveness in conflict is accepting that it is normal."[45] In *Tell It To The Church*, Buzzard and Eck contend; "In many cases conflict is healthy

---

[44] John W. Vale and Robert B. Hughes, *Getting Even: Handling Conflict So That Both Sides Win* (Grand Rapids, MI: Zondervan Publishing House, 1987), 9.

[45] Kreider and Goossen, 11.

23

and necessary."[46] This is particularly true when conflict is understood as being neutral in and of itself as most literature does. John Miller argues that conflict is neutral; "Disagreement doesn't necessitate disharmony, division doesn't necessitate hatred."[47] In other words, how people respond to conflict determines its adverse or beneficial potential.

However, conflict's inevitability can also be explained by understanding the theological, sociological and psychological influence on conflict.

Theological Reasons that Make Conflict Inevitable

A theology of conflict would reveal a consortium of reasons demonstrating conflict's inevitability, three of which will be broadly discussed here: 1) the story of God's creation, 2) the story of man's fall, and 3) the nature of the church and the gospel.

The Story of God's Creation. The seeds of conflict are found in God's creation. His creative diversity, as well as the creation of His image in man—one that encourages creativity

---

[46] Lynn R. Buzzard and Laurence Eck, *Tell It to the Church* (Wheaton, IL: Tyndale House Publishers, 1985), 15.

[47] John M Miller, *The Contentious Community: Constructive Conflict in the Church* (Philadelphia: Westminster Press, 1978), 16.

and permits choice—facilitates conflict. John Lederach uses the "Genesis Window," a perspective on conflict that emerges out of the creation story, to note that "By the very way we are created, conflict will be a part of our ongoing human experience."[48] "The very elements that make human experience rich and dynamic...are the elements that make conflict inevitable. Conflict is natural."[49] Central to this concept is the place conflict plays in God's creation plans. Ron Susek notes, "Real, God-given differences exist in people" including such things as goals, needs, perspectives, values, methods, and interests, none of which are sinful or evil in themselves and must therefore "be respected and honored, as well as blended (which is basic in spiritual growth)...."[50] These "God-given differences" demonstrate His infinite creativity. In discussing the place of conflict in God's creation, Westerhoff states,

> Conflict is not just inevitable .... Instead it is part of the divine plan, a gift. Disruption is integral to God's order. Conflict doesn't sometimes provide us with energy, insight, and new possibility as reluctant by-products; newness cannot come without conflict.

---

[48] John Paul Lederach, *The Journey toward Reconciliation* (Scottdale, PA: Herald Press, 1999), 116.

[49] Ibid.

[50] Susek, 26.

It is not a price to be paid and endured, but a condition to be sought and welcomed and nurtured.[51]

The "energy, insight, and new possibility" that Westerhoff mentions are what many writers have seen as part of the integral connection between conflict and creativity. Donald Bossart elucidates; "What we most often miss in conflict situations is the understanding, the attitude accompanying the skills that make it possible to utilize the dynamics creatively."[52] In a similar vein Marshall Shelly argues that "controlled friction produces energy and energy is essential to creativity."[53] Creativity is both seen in and is a part of the fabric of the universe as a reflection of the character of God. The literature on church conflict suggests that conflict is the spawning bed for creativity, and as such, it is a natural reflection of the ways of God.

Theologically, the inevitability of conflict is made sure in the story of man's fall where we are introduced to Satan, the ultimate source of destructive conflict and its constant instigator and agitator. Strangely, his role in conflict is all but

---

[51] Caroline A. Westerhoff, "Conflict: The Birthing of the New," in *Conflict Management in Congregations*, ed. David B. Lott (Bethesda, MD: Alban Institute, 2001), 56.

[52] Bossart, 229.

[53] Marshall Shelley, *Well-Intentioned Dragons: Ministering to Problem People in the Church* (Waco, TX: Word Books, 1985), 120.

ignored by most of the literature. In *Firestorm*, Susek does include an excellent chapter, "Fire from the Abyss," describing Satan's willing interest in "adding fuel to the firestorm."[54] Typical of most of the literature from the Reconciliation (peacemaking) model, this cosmic dimension of conflict is never far from the discussion.

The Story of Man's Fall. The story of man's fall also reveals the origin of man's sin nature as the product of his rebellion against God. Douglas Lewis warns, "Conflict should not be equated with sin, but our sin nature makes conflict potentially destructive."[55] The initial and immediate consequences of the Fall (Gen 3:15-19) result in conflict that is both cosmic ("And I will put enmity between you (serpent) and the woman"), intrapersonal ("Your desire will be for your husband"), interpersonal ("he will rule over you"), and substantive ("cursed is the ground because of you"). As McSwain states, "Conflict is introduced into every dimension of human reality because of human sin... The source of conflict in the world is this human sin."[56] Not only is conflict introduced in humanity, but in its negative connotation, it is viewed as the inevitable product of man's sin nature as

---

[54] Susek, 106.

[55] Lewis, 40.

[56] McSwain and Treadwell, 21.

evidenced in the "deeds of the flesh" which include "discord," "dissensions," and "factions" along with a host of conflict-producing attitudes and actions (Gal 5:19-21). In evaluating the causes behind the conflict firestorm at Myerstown Grace Brethren Church, the case study of his book, Ron Susek writes,

> The greatest threat to your church is human nature. It underlies all the previous causes we just considered. It generates an endless supply of evil schemes. The well-being of your church will depend upon teaching people to wage a daily war on their own flesh (Rom 6; Eph 4:23), separate from the ways of the world (Isa 52:11), and give no ground of opportunity to Satan (Eph 4:27).[57]

Here Susek brings together several of the components of the story of man's fall that make conflict inevitable as he observed them at work amongst people in a conflicted church—"their own flesh," "the ways of the world," and "opportunity of Satan."

<u>The Nature of the Church and the Gospel</u>. Halverstadt surmises that one reason church conflict turns so destructive is that "parties to church fights profess a gospel that is volatile."[58] The volatility in mind no doubt includes Jesus' indication that He did not come to bring peace but a sword

---

[57] Susek, 105.

[58] Halverstadt, 2.

28

that would set family relationships awry (Matt 10:34, 35).
Speed Leas states, "It is not possible for a church to be
tension-free while being simultaneously faithful to all aspects
of the Law and the Gospel."[59] Thus, faithfulness to the
Gospel makes some form of conflict necessary and therefore
inevitable. Necessity and inevitability presume a sense of
purpose—one not easily deciphered. However, in the
providence of God, conflict serves His purpose. In that sense,
there is an oughtness to it. Lynn Buzzard comments, "I
believe a certain level of ongoing conflict or tension probably
ought to be part of the church...."[60] In his article, "Handling
Holy Wars," Ron Kraybill argues similarly; the "first, and
most important, principle is to allow conflict and even
encourage it."[61] "The question is not whether we disagree
but how we disagree. Jesus assumes there will be conflict
among believers...."[62] Kraybill recognizes conflict's
inevitability, which at its appropriate levels, serves an
immediate theological purpose that benefits the church.
Dudley and Hilgert go so far to say, "A church without

---

[59] Leas, *Moving Your Church through Conflict*, 27.

[60] Lynn Buzzard, "War and Peace in the Local Church,"
Leadership 4:3 (Summer 1983): 21.

[61] Ronald S. Kraybill, "Handling Holy Wars," *Leadership*
7:4 (Fall 1986): 31.

[62] Ibid., 32.

internal conflict is not recognizing its humanity. A church without external conflict is not Christian."[63] What Dudley and Hilgert argue is what Scripture consistently warns; that conflict will of necessity be created by doctrinal dissension and moral corruption from within the church (1 Tim 1:3-7; 4:1-5; 6:3-5; 2 Tim 3:1-5, 2 Tim 4:1-5) and persecution from without (Luke 21:12; John 15:20; Phil 1:29; 2 Tim 4:12; 1 Pet 4:16). Halverstadt summarizes: "While Christian religiosity often operates to preserve the status quo, Christian faithfulness operates to challenge and change the status quo. In itself, such inner conflict between religious security and spiritual risk taking generates emotional conflict between believers."[64]

Sociological Reasons that make Conflict Inevitable

Conflict is also naturally connected to the life of the church because it is a developing societal institution wherein people's needs, beliefs, values, and interrelationships mix. The literature highlights several issues that are particularly relevant to the church; 1) the nature of humanity, 2) the nature of organizations, 3) the Scripture's ideal of community, and 4) unrealistic Christian expectations.

---

[63] Carl S. Dudley and Earle Hilgert, *The New Testament Tensions and the Contemporary Church* (Philadelphia, PA: Fortress Press, 1987), 134.

[64] Halverstadt, 2.

The Nature of Humanity. Human individuality with its beliefs and values makes conflict inevitable. John Miller explains; "It is fantasy to believe there will be no divisions in the church because when you 'care deeply' you defend and fight."[65] Few would argue that "caring deeply" is not crucial to our humanity but may question its conflict-potential. Speed Leas properly observes that "conflict is a function of caring."[66]

The Nature of Organizations. Organizational life demands an element of conflict or tension, and that on several accounts. Peter Steinke affirms the need for conflict in stating, "For any system to be healthy, it has to be challenged; sometimes that challenge comes in the form of conflict."[67] Fred Prinzing's book, *Handling Church Tensions Creatively* focuses on the necessity of tension. He writes; "The existence of tension is a sign of life. When tension ceases to exist, so does the vitality of the church. Our efforts in a local church must not be to eliminate tension but to creatively adjust it so that the church can function properly

---

[65] Miller, 16.

[66] Leas and Kittlaus, *Church Fights: Managing Conflict in the Local Church*, 44.

[67] Peter Steinke, "Outbreak," *Leadership* 18:3 (Summer 1997): 47.

in order to fulfill its purpose."[68] George Barna would assign those "efforts" to "creatively adjust" tension to leadership's responsibility to create conflict and resolve it for the sake of leading the organization towards its purpose.[69] Leadership literature appears to be well aware of the conflict-creativity nexus. Engstrom and Dayton write, "There is a close relationship between conflict and creativity. To avoid conflict is to inhibit creativity.... Conflict then becomes a catalyst to creativity."[70]

It is the movement toward purpose within an organization that is often at conflict's center. Lynn Buzzard states, "If a church ... if it in fact is moving toward something, then there's going to be debate about what that something is and how we get there and who's going to lead us."[71] Mark Galli suggests what that purpose is when he states, "A church without conflict is not merely unimaginable, it also seems to be outside of God's design, for the people of God won't become "the church triumphant" without first being 'the church militant,' and I mean

---

[68] Fred W. Prinzing, *Handling Church Tensions Creatively* (Arlington Heights, IL: Harvest Publications, 1986), 15.

[69] George Barna, *A Fish out of Water* (Brentwood, TN: Integrity Publishers, 2002), 139.

[70] Ted W. Engstrom and Edward R. Dayton, *The Christian Executive* (Waco, TX: Word Books, 1979), 178-179.

[71] Buzzard, "War and Peace in the Local Church," 21.

militant."[72] Without question, the church's purpose and its ensuing goals and strategy have been at the center of many church conflicts as history well testifies.

Regarding as well the important place that conflict plays in the development and sustenance of organizational life, Donald Bossart explains that "societal groups need disharmony and dissociation in order to work out boundaries and identity, as well as harmony and association."[73] The healthy unity that Scripture points to as the experiential goal for its people, is one made more sure and precious through conflict. Thus, Bill Hybels can say, "The mark of community—true biblical unity—is not the absence of conflict. It's the presence of a reconciling spirit."[74] The literature, then, in keeping with the tone of Scripture suggests that unity demands conflict.

The Scripture's Ideal of Community. The inevitability of conflict is elevated by Scripture's ideal of community. It is generally believed by sociologists that conflict (lower levels)

---

[72] Mark Galli, "Epilogue," in *Mastering Conflict and Controversy*, ed. Ed Dobson (Portland, OR: Multnomah Press, 1992), 191.

[73] Bossart, 18.

[74] An Interview with Bill Hybels, "Standing in the Crossfire," *Leadership* 14:1 (Winter 1993): 14.

is the necessary means of building genuine human community.[75] Halverstadt writes,

> Through constructive conflicts Christian catholicity and community are realized. It was through constructive church fights that primitive Christians were able to bridge their differing ethnic, class, linguistic, and religious backgrounds in realizing a oneness in Christ.[76]

Family Systems theorists agree that it is the nature of the church as family that makes conflict unavoidable and normal, making it all the more important to keep "fighting" in the open "where it can be handled fairly and constructively."[77] This is especially true if we consider that the church is the community where God is forming His people. Van Yperen offers some valuable insight; "Church conflict is about character. To redeem character we must be a community of faith being saved and sanctified together in mutual submission under Word and Spirit."[78] The sanctification that Van Yperen speaks of is that which leads to the development of moral character within the community

---

[75] D. Stanley Eitzen and Maxine Baca Zinn, *In Conflict and Order: Understanding Society*, 9th ed. (Boston: Allyn and Bacon, 2001).

[76] Halverstadt, 27.

[77] Cosgrove and Hatfield, 42.

[78] Van Yperen, 63.

of faith, a process and place that makes conflict inevitable. "Communal processes are prevenient in changing individual's consciousness and behaviors."[79]

Additionally, it is the church's nature as being characterized by diversity that also makes conflict inevitable. Ken Sande argues that it is our uniqueness as believers that are part of our God-given differences that make conflict inevitable.[80] It was for conflict over diversity that Paul exhorts the Corinthians through his metaphor of the body to consider the diversity that exists in unity and the unity that exists in diversity (1 Cor 12).

Unrealistic Christian Expectations. Christian's tendency to hold unrealistic expectations about life in the church makes conflict inevitable. Speed Leas aptly summarizes why church conflict is inevitable; "The church hopes for more than other institutions...."[81] But at times, that hope is not founded on reality. Goodman writes,

> Most people believe that the church, after all, should be the one place where brotherly and sisterly love prevails, where other cheeks are turned, where

---

[79] Halverstadt, 28.

[80] Sande, 30.

[81] Speed B. Leas, "The Basics of Conflict Management in Congregations," in *Conflict Management in Congregations*, ed. David B. Lott (Bethesda, MD: Alban Institute, 2001), 20.

people are not judgmental, and where forgiveness flows. Such simplistic expectations may explain why inevitable conflict within congregations is not confronted early and in a healthy manner but is instead allowed to fester and grow.[82]

The answer to dealing with these misplaced hopes and unrealistic expectations is what Halverstadt refers to as "rethinking gut theologies," the "updating of one's habitual, unexamined inner beliefs and ideas with Christian messages."[83] One example is the possibility that a "gut theology" built upon Jesus' words, "Let whoever is without sin cast the first stone," could lead to the assumption that "I have no right to criticize others."[84] From a true biblical perspective, however, the assumption does not necessarily follow. The reality is, as Halverstadt and others demonstrate, that many Christian beliefs about conflict and community in the church are the equivalent to these gut theologies that are feeling-based ideas and assumptions that have not been shaped by Scripture; only caricatures of Scripture.[85] These

---

[82] Denise W. Goodman, *Congregational Fitness* (Bethesda, MD: Alban Institute, 2000), 8.

[83] Halverstadt, 29.

[84] Ibid., 30.

[85] Ibid., 202.

can potentially create a sociological climate that is adverse to normal, healthy responses to conflict. While parishioner's expectations go unmet, conflict is driven underground where its potential for disruption is staggering. Goodman states, "We hope that membership and participation in a faith community will ultimately be a transforming experience. But church doors are not like Etch-a-Sketch slates, automatically erasing all our human flaws when we walk through them."[86]

Psychological Reasons that Make Conflict Inevitable

The presenting issue of most conflict appears as either inter-personal or substantive, but it almost always originates within the inner self making it intrapersonal.

The Intrapersonal Dimension of Faith. The nature of faith and its relationship to the human soul make a degree of religious conflict inevitable. Halverstadt states that "parties' core identities are at risk in church conflicts. Spiritual commitments and faith understandings are highly inflammable because they are central to one's psychological identity."[87] Religious and spiritual differences are often taken personally in that one's worldview and personal

---

[86] Goodman, 9.

[87] Halverstadt, 2.

integrity is questioned or even condemned. This attack on one's "psychological identity" inevitably causes intrapersonal conflict which then exposes itself interpersonally in a variety of attempts of self-justification and self-protection.

The Presence of Psychologically-Damaged People. There are also a number of socio-psychological maladies experienced by humanity in general and church members in particular that seemingly make conflict inevitable. In his discussion of "social pyromaniacs," Ron Susek describes a group of conflicted individuals in today's society including the church who are "emotionally conditioned for pain, not peace."[88] Susek continues to argue that they have become "emotionally conditioned" as the combined result of "destructive family backgrounds" and "unresolved psycho-social needs." The "destructive family backgrounds" include the presence of such negative influences as overbearing fathers, controlling mothers, broken homes, alcoholic parents, abuse, rejection, enmeshment, individualized families, legalistic homes, and libertarian homes.[89] The five "unresolved psycho-social needs" include 1) Acceptance—to be valued, approved and appreciated by those deemed personally important, 2) A Sense of personal achievement—

---

[88] Susek, 82.

[89] Ibid., 83-86.

38

to believe that something of lasting worth has been personally accomplished, 3) A sense of value to a group—to be affirmed and appreciated by the group for valuable contributions, 4) A sense of safety—to feel protected from various personal hazards that jeopardize one's physical, emotional, sociological, and mental health, and 5) A sense of destiny—to believe that progress is being made toward a worthwhile purpose, goal, or destination.[90] The significant point being made here is that those who, for whatever reason, have become "emotionally conditioned for pain," will inevitably act out with disruptive behavior in varying degrees resulting in increasing circles of conflict within the church. Anthony Pappas has captured the painful result; "It is truly said that hurt people hurt people."[91]

The Presence of Behavioral and Interrelational Distortions. In his chapter, "Hazards, Hazards Everywhere," Arthur Boers describes yet another dangerous set of behavioral and interrelational distortions that lead inevitably to conflict: 1) Transference and Countertransference, 2) Projection, 3) Symbolic Role, 4) Pastor's Idealism, 5) Triangulation, 6) Chronic Anxiety, 7) Social Incompetence,

---

[90] Ibid., 86-88.

[91] Anthony G. Pappas, *Pastoral Stress* (Bethesda, MD: Alban Institute, 1995), 47.

39

and 8) Bullying.[92] In his response to these maladies he states,

> There will always be difficult behavior in church.... We can neither change nor avoid the inevitable reality of difficult behavior.... Ignoring or avoiding such problems does not help. They do not go away; often they get worse.[93]

The Scripture's Mandate to Resolve Church Conflict

Church conflict management is also necessary because Scripture mandates that the church resolve its conflict and experience the unity and peace found in Christ and His Spirit (John 17:20-23; Eph 4:3). As central as this seems, few sources in church conflict management develop it. Those whose approach it from a Reconciliation (peacemaking) perspective will most naturally, as Dave Peters contends, hear the injunctions of Scripture regarding the pursuit of peace as divine mandates, as biblical exhortations to be reconciled to God and the family of God through repentance and forgiveness.[94] Peter's book, *Surviving Church Conflict*, along with Ken Sande's *The Peacemaker* and Van Yperen's *Making Peace* are the

---

[92] Boers, 32-56.

[93] Ibid., 57.

[94] Dave Peters, *Surviving Church Conflict* (Scottdale, PA: Herald Press, 1997), 46-47.

exception. Van Yperen, for example, notes that Scripture frequently exhorts the church to the business of peacemaking. As an example, he refers to Paul's appeal to the Corinthians and his pleading of Euodia and Syntyche to get to the business of agreement in the Lord—a peacemaking mission.[95] He also notes that the church has been given the central role in conflict management by way of its unique giftedness; "Discipline and discernment are given to the church to discern God's will and to work out reconciliation."[96]

In *Surviving Church Conflict* Peters offers four reasons why it is necessary for the church to participate in the resolution of conflict: 1) Love of the gospel compels the church to desire restored fellowship for all its members (Matt 5:44), 2) The desire for obedience compels the church to become involved no matter how difficult the situation (Matt 18), 3) Love of the sinner compels the church to rescue the perishing (Luke 15), and 4) Love of the truth compels the church to seek to turn sinners from their error (James 5:19-20).[97] Peters also refers to the church's moral imperative, that is, the foundation upon which all biblical peacemaking rests is the understanding that God has made peace through

---

[95] Van Yperen, 171.

[96] Ibid., 182.

[97] Peters, 118-121.

the blood of the cross (Col 1:20).[98] Jesus' ministry of reconciliation makes church conflict management, understood in its broadest terms, necessary. Peters sees the need for conflict management at even a more cosmic level: "Peacemaking is the call to spiritual obedience in the conflicts between two spiritual kingdoms."[99] The stakes of church conflict management are high when viewed from this spiritual dimension.

---

[98] Ibid., 45.

[99] Ibid., 55.

The Elements of Diagnosis in Church Conflict Management

The literature clearly demonstrates a need for church conflict management, especially in light of conflict's inevitability and Scripture's call for peace and unity within the faith community. Essential to any theory of conflict management is the development of systems and structures that assist managers in diagnosing conflict so that the appropriate skills and strategies can be employed. Though many tools have been utilized, the literature frequently refers to the "types," "levels," "sources," and orientations of conflict as being particularly useful to diagnosis in conflict management.

The Types of Church Conflict

All conflict is classified into "types"—what it is about. The literature classifies conflict in a few categories, the broadest of which is personality-centered and principle-centered, a distinction carefully discussed by Huttenlocker in *Conflict and Caring.*[100]

---

[100] Keith Huttenlocker, *Conflict and Caring: Preventing, Managing, and Resolving Conflict in the Church* (Grand Rapids, MI: Ministry Resources Library, 1988), 83-92.

Interpersonal or Personal-Centered Conflict

Personal-centered conflict has been generally identified as "interpersonal," that which focuses on issues pertaining to personality, power, recognition, and communication styles to name a few. Leas states, "This conflict is not generated by what a person does or what he thinks ... but by how he feels about the other person."[101]

Substantive or Principle-Centered Conflict

Principle-centered conflict is more frequently called "substantive" conflict. Leas and Kittlaus, following the model of Tannenbaum and Schmidt, have distinguished four kinds of substantive conflict: 1) facts—disagreement over information, 2) methods—differences over procedures, strategies, or tactics in achieving a solution to a problem, 3) ends or goals—what should be accomplished, and 4) values and beliefs—differences in life philosophy and worldview. ("The Management of Differences," in *Leadership and Organization*).[102] An example of substantive conflict can be seen in Peter Steinke's list of ten "anxiety triggers": 1) money, 2) sex and sexuality, 3) styles of worship, 4) old and new (ex. leaders, curriculum, members), 5) internal vs.

---

[101] Leas and Kittlaus, *Church Fights: Managing Conflict in the Local Church*, 31.

[102] Leas, "The Basics of Conflict Management in Congregations," 24-25.

external focus (ex. foreign missions vs. home ministry), 6) pastoral leadership style, 7) staff conflict, 8) growth and survival issues, 9) sudden death of a child, 10) trauma or transition (e.g., a pastor who retires after thirty-five years).[103] The anecdotal material of most of the literature refers to one or more of these issues. Additionally, much of the literature based on a managerial, administrative approach assumes that substantive issues are foundational to conflict.[104]

Intrapersonal Conflict

Additionally, some conflict, more peripheral to the church, is intrapersonal—the struggle a person has within himself, issues related to self-identity and esteem. Most literature exhorts pastors caught up in conflict to face it first within themselves, i.e., intrapersonally.[105] In his book, *The Other Side of Leadership*, Eugene Habecker discusses the four responsibilities of leadership in conflict, the most important being that "leaders need to be continually involved

---

[103] Peter Steinke, "Top Ten Anxiety Triggers," *Leadership* 18:3 (Summer 1997): 48.

[104] Leas, *Moving Your Church through Conflict*.

[105] Monty Burnham and others, "Leadership Forum. Conflict: Facing It in Yourself and in Your Church," *Leadership* 1:2 (Spring 1980): 23-28.

in self-confrontation, using God's Word as their standard."[106] This is pertinent since most church conflict becomes interpersonal regardless of how it started. A recent Leadership survey indicated that 71 percent of the time, the pastor becomes the focus of the conflict.[107] Thus, his ability to separate himself (his feelings, identity, esteem) from the conflict is crucial to his ability to manage it.

Systemic Conflict

Still others, especially those who approach conflict from a Family Systems theory would juxtapose individual conflict against that of the group. Central to the development of Freidman's Family Systems approach to conflict management is the belief that conflict is not an individual problem, but a systemic one in which the dysfunction of the church family is responsible for personal intransigence and nonconformity.[108] The literature demonstrates an increasing awareness that difficult behavior and tendencies for conflict are integrally connected to the larger social unit—the church as family.

---

[106] Eugene B. Habecker, *The Other Side of Leadership* (Wheaton, IL: Victor Books, 1987), 99.

[107] Reed: 25.

[108] Edwin H. Friedman, *Generation to Generation: Family Process in Church and Synagogue* (New York, NY: The Guilford Press, 1985).

Peters views conflict more cosmically—within the church between "Christian believers," and in the world where "Christians are "deliberately persecuted for their faith."[109] In *Surviving Church Conflict,* he sees the inbreaking of the kingdom of God through Jesus' ministry as "eternal conflict resolution." Van Yperen argues similarly but more forcefully that church conflict is always theological, never merely interpersonal.[110]

The Levels/Stages of Church Conflict

A discussion of the levels of conflict will naturally focus on Speed Leas whose work in the field of conflict management, particularly of the levels of conflict, is foundational for much of the literature. Thus, this section will rely almost exclusively on his conflict management manual, *Moving Your Church through Conflict,* his only book that actually includes a full discussion of this aspect of conflict management theory.

The utilization of levels of conflict helps categorize the severity of conflict, helping to determine the level of concern and response to be expended. The determination of the "levels" of conflict is based upon the nature of the language used by the parties involved and, by their goals/objectives.

---

[109] Peters, 96-117.

[110] Van Yperen, 24.

The increase in levels is marked by language augmented by intensity, distortion, and generalization, while goals become more self-centered and diffused. Level I represents "Problems to Solve" in which the conflicted are characterized by an attitude that is problem-oriented, a desire to fix the problem, and language (speech/communication) that is engaging, open, descriptive and collaborative. Level II represents "Disagreements" in which the parties involved become more concerned with self-protection than problem-solving. Language is marked by generalization, calculation, caution and mistrust. Level III, "Contest," presumes a win/lose orientation in which the parties' goals have shifted from self-protection to winning which generally includes the formation of factions. Language distorts their opponent's views and is characterized by magnification, dichotomization, over-generalization and assumption. Level IV, "Fight/Flight," continues the win/lose orientation but shifts in its goals to wanting to hurt or get rid of the opponent. Factions become coalitions where strong leaders emerge who exploit concepts such as truth, righteousness and justice with idealized language. Level V has been labeled, "Intractable Solutions" because it is "conflict run amok." The goal of opponents is to destroy the other for the sake of an eternal cause they are willing to fight and die for.[111]

---

[111] Leas, *Moving Your Church through Conflict*, 9-16.

The practicality of understanding these levels of conflict is articulated in Leas' three assumptions: "Not all conflict is the same; One's 'gut reaction' is not a reliable indicator of the actual level of difficulty; Responses to conflict should be adjusted to the level of difficulty."[112] Much of the literature has taken these assumptions to heart by including Leas' levels of conflict as part of their management strategies.

In a similar but metaphorical way, Ron Susek has utilized language describing the life cycle of a firestorm to describe the "phases" of conflict by way of its intensity: Phase 1—Sparks, Phase 2—Sparks Igniting a Firestorm, Phase 3—Firestorm in Full Fury, Phase 4 —Consuming Winds, and Phase 5—The Final Burn.[113] Susek goes to considerable length following the discussion of each phase to explain the natural dynamics at work, descriptions that sound peculiarly similar to those depicted by Leas.

The Sources of Church Conflict

In outlining the sources of church conflict, the literature seldom differentiates between sources, causes, and reasons for conflict. What is clear, however, despite the ambiguous terminology, is that ultimate and penultimate

---

[112] Ibid., 17.

[113] Susek, 15-59.

sources are in view. Most of the literature focuses on penultimate sources and finds significant agreement in their identity. Few writers consider conflict's ultimate source, and that with some disagreement.

The Penultimate Sources of Conflict

Roy Pneuman's chapter in *Conflict Management in Congregations*, "Nine Common Sources of Conflict in Congregations," is a compendium of his work as a senior consultant for the Alban Institute. His list is indicative of the causes/reasons for church conflict found in much of the literature: 1) people disagree about values and beliefs, 2) the structure is unclear, 3) the pastor's role and responsibilities are conflictual, 4) the structure no longer fits the congregations' size, 5) the clergy and parish leadership styles don't match, 6) the new pastor rushes into changes, 7) communication lines are blocked, 8) church people manage conflict poorly, and 9) disaffected members hold back participation and pledges.[114] In a sense, from a psychological/counseling framework, these causes of conflict often function as the "presenting issue" of deeper trouble—

---

[114] Roy W. Pneuman, "Nine Common Sources of Conflict in Congregations," in *Conflict Management in Congregations*, ed. David B. Lott (Bethesda, MD: Alban Institute, 2001), 45-53.

the surface issue that draws attention to the fact that people feel bad about something.[115]

Donald Bossart, following the work of sociologist Morton Deutsch, sees church conflict originating from, 1) control over resources, 2) preferences—nuisances which can merge intoi a struggle for power, 3) values—what 'should be," 4) beliefs about what really is, and 5) nature of relationships between parties, such as over-dominance or togetherness" (*The Resolution of Conflict*, 15-17).[116] Family systems theorists include these issues as capable of intensifying conflict: "the loss of a long-tenured pastor, a series of short term pastorates, a traumatic incident in the church, poorly defined structures or policies, building programs, sexual boundary-crossing by clergy, a membership decrease or increase, tensions within the denomination, and a restructure or reorganization."[117]

Fred Prinzing uses anecdotal material to discuss culturally sensitive issues that create tension in the church such as home vs. world missions, evangelism vs. social gospel, structure vs. spontaneity. He contends that there are at least seven timeless causes of conflict in the church. These

---

[115] Leas, "Inside Church Fights: An Interview with Speed Leas," 13.

[116] Bossart, 17.

[117] Friedman, 203-204.

include differences in culture, generations, leadership, theology, spirituality, personal preferences, and priorities.[118]

Many writers have sought to create clearer, broader classifications for conflict. McSwain and Treadwell offer the following: 1) attitudes—differences of perspectives about persons and issues, 2) substantive issues—differences of opinions about facts, goals, ends, or means, 3) emotions— when personal value is attached to either attitudinal or substantive issues, and 4) communication—a breakdown in healthy, open conversation.[119]

Van Yperen, using a more biblically-centered approach, claims there are four systemic issues at the root of conflict: cultural syncretism, unhealthy church structure, spiritual pathology, and theological confusion regarding the nature of the church.[120] The multiplication of such lists highlights the complexity of conflict management. Thus, many evangelicals would likely agree with Van Yperen's assessment: "Conflict is always a complex interaction of cultural, structural, spiritual, and theological forces. Most conflict surfaces and displays interpersonal symptoms that

---

[118] Prinzing, 208-211.

[119] McSwain and Treadwell, 25-26.

[120] Van Yperen, 28-46.

have underlying systemic, theological roots."[121] Van Yperen
has drawn closer to realizing conflict's ultimate source.

The Ultimate Sources of Conflict

As mentioned, there seems to be little agreement
within the literature regarding ultimate sources of conflict.

Stress and Fear as Conflict's Ultimate Source

Malony advocates seeing "stress" as the root cause of
conflict.[122] McSwain and Treadwell agree stating that, "The
person experiencing stress within is the root of conflict with
others."[123] As this statement indicates, they understand
stress to be intrapersonal conflict in which a perceived threat
(actual or anticipated) is experienced from the realms of the
physical (physical injury, pain or death), ego (injury to the
psychological self), interpersonal (a disruption of social
relationships), environmental (financially constraint or
impoverishment), or spiritual (disruption of practices which
promote a sense of the presence of God in one's life).[124]
Within the same model of conflict management, Speed Leas,

---

[121] Ibid., 46.

[122] Malony, *Win-Win Relationships: 9 Strategies for
Settling Personal Conflict without Waging War*, 43-46.

[123] McSwain and Treadwell, 60.

[124] Ibid., 58.

though questioning whether the causes of conflict can be known, argues from physiology that fear—that innate, primitive, initiatory survival response to any perceived threat—motivates and prepares the individual for conflict.[125] Thus, it is the reduction of fear that is conflict management's first subgoal.[126]

Diversity within the Church as Conflict's Ultimate Source

In Rumford's inter-personal conflict approach, he states that the ultimate source of conflict is diversity in the Body.[127] Horace Fenton acknowledges this potential for conflict, but finds within it more specific causes: "Different perspectives, different goals, different experiences will lead us to different conclusions, even when brothers and sisters share the same basic tenets of our faith."[128] But these suggest penultimate causes founded in substantive issues. It has already been argued that diversity represents a potential for

---

[125] Leas, *Moving Your Church through Conflict*, 9.

[126] Ibid., 10.

[127] Douglas J. Rumford, "Cacophony or Symphony," *Leadership* 7:4 (Fall 1986): 97-98.

[128] Horace L. Fenton, Jr., *When Christians Clash* (Downers Grove, IL: InterVarsity Press, 1987), 109.

conflict. But a "potential" for conflict, however, is not likely to be conflict's "source."

Power as Conflict's Ultimate Source

John Wallace's book, *Control in Conflict*, suggests that power could be the root of conflict. He states; "Conflict is intrinsically related to power. Every conflict involves the use of power."[129] Wallace contends that power's abuse causes conflict: 1) the abuse of power—power used for self-centered endeavors, 2) the assignment of power—disruption created over the empowerment of individuals, 3) the assumption of power—when individuals suppose it is their prerogative to claim power, and 4) the absence of power—when individuals seek to gain control where power vacuums exist.[130] This position has much to commend it considering how much attention is given to the subject of the use of and response to power and authority in the teachings of Jesus and the Apostles.

Spiritual Depravity as Conflict's Ultimate Source

Conflict management models representing a Scripture-based peacemaking approach basically agree that

---

[129] John Wallace, *Control in Conflict* (Nashville, TN: Broadman Press, 1982), 47.

[130] Ibid., 47-48.

the ultimate source of conflict is spiritual in nature—rooted deeply in man's sin nature. Invariably, James 4:1 is quoted; "What causes fights and quarrels among you? Don't they come from your desires that battle within you?" Evangelicals would rightly contend that, based particularly on Pauline theology, the inner battles James speaks of are centered in the Flesh (Rom 7). Marshall Shelley reminds us that "people can't overcome their human nature…. The church is made up of self-sacrificing saints and self-serving sinners."[131] Miller and Form state that conflict arises because of "unvarnished human cussedness" and "sinful cantankerousness,"[132] a rather descript way of alluding to man's depravity. Following three chapters of analysis in the "human factors" that cause destructive conflict, Ron Susek admits that they are all only contributory and point to an underlying cause:

> Here's the point: The greatest threat to your church is human nature. It underlies all the previous causes we just considered. It generates an endless supply of evil schemes. The well-being of your church will largely depend upon teaching people to wage a daily war on their own flesh (Romans 6; Eph. 4:23), separate from the ways of the world (Isa. 52:11), and give no ground of opportunity to Satan (Eph. 4:27).[133]

---

[131] Shelley, 48.

[132] Miller, 22.

[133] Susek, 106.

The Practice of Church Conflict Management

Douglas Lewis asserts that "Organizational research reveals that the most effective organizations are ones that develop processes for managing conflict."[134] It not surprising then, that the literature on church conflict unanimously agrees that conflict management is necessary. Previously it has been shown why conflict management is necessary. This is not to say of course, that the Church at large agrees or that it knows how. Thus, the literature on church conflict deals predominantly with management processes and the strategies capable of directing the conflict situation toward its potential benefits while seeking to avoid its potential dangers.

Definitions of "Church Conflict Management"

This process is generally reflected in how conflict management is defined and described. Shawchuck states: "Church conflict management is the process of influencing the actions and attitudes of an individual or group in the midst of disagreement, tensions, and behavioral actions which are threatening the relationship and or the

---

[134] Lewis, 24.

accomplishment of goals.[135] True to the basic definitions of conflict, Shawchuck includes the relational and relevance dimensions along with conflict's primary elements. Halverstadt defines conflict management as a "process of intentionally intervening by proposing constructive processes by which to deal with differences," which he further describes as "coping constructively with parties by constraining those who fight dirty and/or assisting those who fight fair."[136] McSwain and Treadwell view conflict management as conflict ministry, offering a definition more suitable to that perspective, but less technical; it as "a process for keeping alive the hope of fulfilled promises ... becoming involved with people at the point of their pain, sinfulness, and meanness."[137] All definitions recognize that conflict management is, 1) an intentional process, 2) directed towards conflicted parties, 3) seeking to positively influence the outcome, and 4) prepared to use various strategies appropriate to the situation. What is patently missing, however, is a clear purpose or end result that can be objectively measured and evaluated.

---

[135] Norman Shawchuck, *How to Manage Conflict in the Church* (Irvine, CA: Spiritual Growth Resources, 1983), 21.

[136] Halverstadt, 10.

[137] McSwain and Treadwell, 15.

The Practitioners of Church Conflict Management

The thesis of *Spiritual Maturity: Preserving Congregational Health and Balance*, is that leadership is a "healing modality," that is, it is the catalyst that continuously forces the congregation to deal with its dissent and disagreement by handling it "directly and forthrightly so the church can stay on track to accomplish its mission."[138] In most cases the center figure in leadership will be the pastor. In a section entitled, "Who Manages Conflict?" Lewis answers, "Yes, like it or not, that is one of their chief tasks.... The pastor, whether effective or not, is the primary manager in the system."[139]

Leas and Kittlaus, however, question the effectiveness of pastoral mediated church conflict stating that most ministers, 1) wrongly perceive reconciliation as the absence of conflict, 2) have invariably already taken a position on the issue in question, and 3) have already been implicated by one or both of the parties as being part of the problem.[140] Though this position is widely accepted within the managerial approach to conflict management, writers from the Family-

---

[138] Frank A. Thomas, *Spiritual Maturity: Preserving Congregational Health and Balance* (Minneapolis, MN: Fortress Press, 2002), 91-92.

[139] Lewis, 19-20.

[140] Leas and Kittlaus, *Church Fights: Managing Conflict in the Local Church*, 74.

systems theory view the pastor as necessarily pivotal to any resolution process. As the church family's father, his "strategic participation" utilizes the carefully selected intervening strategies to help its members adjust and cope with conflict.[141] Likewise, those within the Reconciliation model (peacemaking) approach frequently devote entire book sections to the pastoral role in dealing with conflict.[142] Peters, for example, offers to pastors, five *guidelines* for dealing with divided congregations, three *concerns* he must attend to in restoring church cohesiveness, and eighteen *actions* he must take in negotiating conflict resolution.[143] Additionally, Arthur Boer's *Never Call Them Jerks*, is a pastoral handbook on conflict management. Its final three chapters focuses explicitly on what responsible leadership in the midst of conflict looks like, offering keen insight into the pastor's responsibility to deal with differentiation, confrontation, and self-awareness and self- examination.[144]

Where the pastor fails to meet the criteria of officiating a church fight, or when the situation either includes the pastor or has gone beyond his ability to control, most of the literature advises the use of professionals

---

[141] Cosgrove and Hatfield, 126-127.

[142] Peters, 47-54.; Boers, 93-107.

[143] Peters, 47-51.

[144] Boers, 92-133.

specializing in conflict resolution. Leas and Kittlaus offer these suggestions for qualifications of a "referee": 1) He doesn't take substantive conflict personally, 2) he has a high tolerance for ambiguity, ambivalence and frustration, 3) He is confident in conflict management and refereeing, 4) He is not an advocate for any particular solution, nor does he take sides on the issues in this conflict, 5) he is credible to both (all) sides.[145]

Whether it is the pastor, a professional conflict consultant, or some other third party functioning as a referee, what the literature agrees on is that the leadership of the church must take responsibility for conflict and do so proactively. Peter Steinke warns in this regard that pastoral leaders can be the ruin or the salvation of their church.[146]

The Orientation of Church Conflict

Orientation refers to the way in which conflict is approached from the beginning in how one chooses to relate to the other party with the end in view. Literature from all approaches utilizes an understanding of orientation in its discussion of conflict management, due in part because it informs how the process will be handled.

---

[145] Leas and Kittlaus, *Church Fights: Managing Conflict in the Local Church*, 65-67.

[146] Peter L. Steinke, *Healthy Congregations: A Systems Approach* (Bethesda, MD: Alban Institute, 1996), 99.

Johnson and Johnson have made prominent a two orientation approach to conflict: win/win and win/lose.[147] Win/win is often times labeled as cooperative and constructive (Leas), problem-solving (Willimon), convergence (Bossart), proactive (McSwain and Treadwell), synergistic (Hall), empowering (Wallace), peacemaking (Sande) and others. A Win/win orientation, as described by Johnson and Johnson, 1) defines conflict as a mutual problem, 2) anticipates participation from all parties involved, 3) encourages assertiveness in communication, 4) surfaces and discusses underlying assumptions, 5) handles disagreement as a normal response rather than a personal attack, 6) delineates differences of position as well as similarities so that they can be understood and integrated into the resolution process, 7) permits and accepts communication at an emotional level, 8) views members as holding equal situational power, and 9) tolerates moderate levels of tension.[148] The Win/lose orientation embodies the exact converse to each of these characteristics and need not be listed here. Secular conflict management theory has seemingly embraced this general orientation toward conflict, but it has found disfavor within church conflict management

---

[147] David Johnson and Frank P. Johnson, *Joining Together: Group Theory and Group Skills* (Englewood Cliffs, NJ: Prentice Hall, 1975), 157.

[148] Ibid., 157.

circles, predominantly because there appear to be other biblically acceptable alternatives.

One such approach, which is both complimentary and supplementary to that of Johnson and Johnson, is the one popularized by Jay Hall's *Conflict Management Survey*. Built upon his two-dimensional model of conflict management—context, the concern for relationships, and personal relevance, the concern for personal goals—these are placed on a horizontal and vertical axis creating five styles (orientations) of conflict management. Each reflects its own "system of values" and each results in "different consequences in terms of conflict dynamics."[149] Hall labels these five styles, 9/1 win-lose—the use of power, persuasion and influence in conflict so that "right" (goals, means, values) prevails, 1/9 yield-lose—the acquiescence to other's agendas so that relationship can be preserved, 1/1 lose-leave—the complete withdrawal from conflict accompanied by "impersonal tolerance" for relationships and compliance to goal expectations, 5/5 compromise—the attempt to serve the "common good" by ameliorating differences and bargaining for mutual concessions, 9/9 synergistic—the engaging in aggressive conflict resolution on the assumption

---

[149] Hall, 14-15.

that goals must be adequately served in order for relationships to endure.[150]

Other writers have in some way or another embraced Hall's orientation but labeled them differently. In his book, Preaching about Conflict in the Local Church, William Willimon suggests these "five" styles in conflict management: 1) Problem-Solver—doesn't fear conflict (9/9), 2) Super-Helper—enmeshed with the conflicted (1/9), 3) Power-Broker—chooses goals over relationships (9/1), 4) Facilitator—an adaptive compromiser (5/5), and 5) Fearful Loser—runs from conflict (1/1).[151] In a more creative vein, Shawchuck and Moeller, following corporate psychologists' labeling mechanism for survival responses, have attached these five management styles to animals: 'sharks ("I win; you lose"), foxes ("Everyone wins a little and loses a little"), turtles ("I withdraw"), teddy bears ("I'll lose so you can win"), and owls ("Let's find a way for everyone to win").'[152] The relationship to Hall's model is again perfectly apparent.

These models of orientation towards conflict management are not to be viewed absolutely but rather as personal preferences. They are part of what Hall refers to as

---

[150] Ibid., 16-17.

[151] William H. Willimon, *Preaching About Conflict in the Local Church* (Philadelphia: Westminster Press, 1987), 84-92.

[152] Norman Shawchuck and Robert Moeller, "Animal Instincts," *Leadership* 14:1 (Winter 1993): 44.

a "response hierarchy" which assumes that, though all orientations will be used in some particular context, each individual (and organization) develops a dominant style and preferred order in resorting to the others.[153] Thus, though the 9/9 synergistic orientation is the ideal, the other four represent appropriate backup systems in varying situations.

The Approaches to Church Conflict Management

In discussing the approaches to church conflict management, the central question being asked is, "How can church conflict be managed or resolved?" The literature unveils only a few distinct models; some of which have been heavily influenced by Speed Leas, the pioneer in church management theory. Thus, Lyndel Moe chooses to use Leas' five-level model as the foil against which he can compare the alternative power model.[154] Other conflict management models exist, such as the Family-systems model as well as the Reconciliation model. These models and their representative strategies will be discussed under the follow subheadings: prevention, containment, and resolution of church conflict. This approach to discussing the voluminous material on church conflict management has been chosen as

---

[153] Hall, 17.

[154] Moe, "A Comparison of Two Analytical Models for Understanding Local Church Conflict", 67-79.

an organizing principle because they more clearly identify the ends to which many of the models work.

The Prevention of Church Conflict Management

Much of the literature deals with conflict prevention only indirectly. But several writers have made positive contributions to this pragmatic form of conflict management.

Promote Healthy Communication within the Body. Learned conflict management strategies and skills work to prevent conflict. Edwards and Brandon recommend that the best way to stop church splits is to educate the membership to avoid divisive behavior.[155] Such a simplistic solution has merit, but requires a positive church culture where people are trained to deal with conflict. This is the essence of what Cosgrove and Hatfield argue; that the pastor devises strategies for nurturing the system, focusing on developing and modeling good communication and the understanding and appreciation of authority structures in the church family.[156] Arthur Boers suggests this can be done by promoting healthy responses to difficult behavior such as: 1) promoting respectful behavior that avoids the extremes of

---

[155] Edwards and Brandon.

[156] Cosgrove and Hatfield, 123-176.

"hardball—rigid and harsh approaches) and "softball"—
yielding and enabling reactions, 2) building a "sense of
coherence"—the church perceives that it has meaning, has
control over what happens, and understands the process of
mutual growth, 3) identifying strategies appropriate to the
level of conflict brought by difficult behavior, 4) establishing
"family rules", norms that guide appropriate behavior and
include sanctions when violated, 5) developing guidelines for
"fair fighting"—healthy ways of dealing with ongoing, normal
differences, 6) instituting and enforcing grievance
procedures—an established process that provides guided
oversight to conflictive parties, 7) forming support/listening
teams that help deescalate conflict by allowing conflicted
parties to ventilate their frustrations but holding them
accountable to "family rules."[157]

Encourage Healthy Conflict within the Body. Conflict
prevention occurs when low level conflict is encouraged. Ron
Kraybill asserts, "If you want fewer divisive and church-
splitting conflicts, encourage more everyday disagreements
in congregational life."[158] Similarly, Denise Goodman
suggests that pastors "repeal the 'no-talk' rules" by

---

[157] Boers, 65-79.

[158] Ronald S. Kraybill, *Repairing the Breach* (Scottdale, PA: Herald Press, 1981), 19.

encouraging greater freedom in "raising uncomfortable issues."[159] In his chapter, "Tension Isn't All Bad," Speed Leas suggests six ways to encourage good conflict: 1) Preach about low-level conflict—educate people about conflict, 2) Praise disagreement—it can enhance church life, 3) Mix up committees with people representing differing perspectives, 4) Put newcomers on leadership boards—they see things differently, 5) Set standards for the work of the church— honestly seek feedback and assessment, and 6) Make clear the rules of healthy conflict .[160]

<u>Create a Reconciling Environment within the Body.</u> Hugh Halverstadt advocates three behavioral standards for body-life: 1) personal assertiveness—to love others as oneself recognizing "a common intrinsic worth to all parties," 2) respect for others' rights— "interpersonal respect," and 3) sharing assertiveness for the common good—the goal of a reconciling environment is the edification of the Body.[161] These behaviors require a healthy environment, one that Steinke describes as a "sense of coherence":

---

[159] Goodman, 49-58.

[160] Edward G. Dobson, S. B. Leas, and M. Shelley, *Mastering Conflict and Controversy* (Portland, OR: Multnomah Press, 1992), 38-39.

[161] Halverstadt, 37-38.

A disposition or orientation to life: all the parts of one's life are connected, something ties all people together, and life coheres in a meaningful way. This sense of coherence gives people a compass, builds confidence that the person can positively influence the outcome.[162]

Steinke goes on to describe the three primary ingredients that describe a congregation's sense of coherence: 1) meaningfulness—a congregation believes its actions have meaning and worth, 2) manageability—a congregation believes it has some control and influence over outcomes, 3) comprehensibility—the congregation understands the challenges and knows how to move toward health.[163] In chapters entitled, "The Best Defense," and "The Second Best Defense," Marshall Shelley likewise argues that "Taking opportunities to build a close, cohesive church will produce better results than the shrewdest political maneuvers after problems sprout. Defusing potential problems before they arise is far better than troubleshooting later on."[164] Thus, Shelley offers the following principles for building church health: 1) Encourage a Positive Atmosphere—this breeds advocates not adversaries, 2) Full Employment in People

---

[162] Steinke, *Healthy Congregations: A Systems Approach,* 27-28.

[163] Ibid., 28-31.

[164] Shelley, 83.

Ministries—to involve the laity in meaningful, fulfilling, significant work suppresses attitudes that lead to conflict, 3) Reinforcing Productive Members—focus attention on those involved in productive ministry by spending time with them and honoring them, 4) Knowing Congregational Values—fully understand what has transpired in a congregation and join what the Holy Spirit is already doing, 5) Sharing Outside Interests—participate in life away from business and share it with others outside the office, 6) Underselling Beats Overselling—realize that the church's identity and purpose cannot appeal to everyone, 7) Building a Healthy Board—develop a cohesive group of leaders capable of modeling health and "fighting infectious attitudes" within the Body.[165] These "best" and "second best" defensive measures facilitate what Family-systems theorist, Peter Steinke describes as "eustress"—the promotion of health rather than "distress"—the enabling of disease.[166] The goal of course, is the creation of a healthy community, not one devoid of problems, but one in which they can be creatively and positively dealt with.

Identifying the Early Warning Signs of Conflict. Conflict prevention also assumes that potentially conflictive

---

[165] Ibid., 81-105.

[166] Steinke, *Healthy Congregations: A Systems Approach*, 29.

issues and situations can be identified and ameliorated. This supports Leas and Kittlaus' truism: "conflict properly managed is conflict continuously managed."[167] Leas warns, however, that "we cannot accurately identify all precursors to organizational conflict. We do know some of the things that accompany conflict or that frequently precede disruptive conflict in the church...."[168] Having said that, he discusses eight such warning signs: : 1) environmental factors—external issues such as severe economic hardships, 2) special congregational factors—internal issues such as the departure of a long-tenured pastor, 3) rumors—the voicing of vague and general complaints about most anything that is bothering people, 4) reduced participation—the "withdrawal of personal contact between members," 5) decline in attendance and giving, 6) changes in lay leadership—the establishment of new and challenging authorities, 7) the emergence of "hardliners"—individuals taking adamant positions on issues, and 8) changes in pastor's behavior—the use of coping techniques by the pastor to relieve personal tension.[169] Additionally Leas states that "Pastors know that church conflict is coming. Knowing when it's apt to come is a different matter and one that pastors are wise to be alert

---

[167] Willimon, 19.

[168] Leas, *Moving Your Church through Conflict*, 13.

[169] Ibid., 13-15.

to."[170] From the observations of his experience as a church conflict consultant he contributes a chapter entitled, "The Ten Most Predictable Times of Conflict" in *Mastering Conflict and Controversy*.[171] The literature has become increasingly aware that potentially conflictive issues and situations can be identified through well established warning signs and predictable times of conflict. These can be useful in diagnosis and treatment before conflict engulfs the congregation.

<u>Creating a Purpose-Driven Church Ministry</u>. Purpose-driven ministry and leadership help prevent conflict. Church leaders recognize that catering to parishioner's preferences is organizationally unhealthy and spiritually irresponsible. "Rather than trying to solve problems and fix the causes of complaints, leaders ...trying to manage differences and make decisions based on the congregation's defined purpose or goals."[172] Rendle argues that the energy spent in trying to "fix" congregations by seeking to satisfy each demand is better spent in "managing differences" for the actual purpose of "preserving" them

---

[170] Dobson, Leas, and Shelley, 109.

[171] Ibid., 110-118.

[172] Gil Rendle, "The Illusion of Congregational 'Happiness'," in *Conflict Management in Congregations*, ed. David B. Lott (Bethesda, MD: Alban Institute, 2001), 86.

rather than "harmonizing" or "negotiating" them into common agreement—a daunting task without a clear sense of organizational purpose.[173]

Purposeful Non-confrontation. Preventative conflict management is also realized by knowing when not to confront. Armstrong suggests handling "no-win" conflict situations with "friendly neglect," "going the extra mile," and "playing your position"—three ways to "finesse" conflict that need not be taken to trial.[174] Conversely, in conflict situations controlled by antagonists, as described in "Wars You Can't Win," Bustanoby offers "signs of a no-win war" that preempt destructive conflict; "we should turn over scorched earth to determined terrorists" trusting God's sovereignty over His church.[175]

The Containment of Church Conflict

When conflict reaches level II and III, preventative management techniques must give way to conflict containment strategies. The literature offers several approaches.

---

[173] Ibid., 89.

[174] Leroy R. Armstrong, Jr., "When Not to Confront," *Leadership* 14:1 (Winter 1993): 73-74.

[175] Andre Bustanoby, "Wars You Can't Win," *Leadership* 14:1 (Winter 1993): 63.

Speed Leas' Approach to Conflict Containment. Much of the conflict reduction discussion in the literature focuses around the use of Speed Leas' model that advocates identifying conflict's intensity at one of five levels. The objective is to deescalate conflict to lower levels, preferably level II (Disagreements) or I (Predicaments) that are considered normal and healthy for church life but still require proactive management. Leas suggests three ways to reduce Level III conflict to Level II or I. First, increase the amount of clear, direct communication between the parties—encourage them to express their concerns face to face. Second, help the parties explore areas of agreement—find common ground and possible ways of "advancing their concerns." Third, help the parties discover the deeper interest—look past incompatibilities to deeper unarticulated interests where solutions may yet exist.[176] The focus of these conflict-containing-strategies is relational. In Leas' five-level model, the conflicted parties' use of language becomes a clue to diagnosing conflict's severity. At level III, language no longer focuses on the goals of the group but becomes interpersonally hostile. Thus, strategies at this level focus on restoring relational civility so that constructive interaction can be maintained.

---

[176] Dobson, Leas, and Shelley, 90-91.

The Managerial/Communications Approach to Conflict Containment. Gangel and Canine, representing a managerial communications approach to conflict management, organize tactics into four categories; avoidance, escalation, maintenance, and reduction. These can be used positively or negatively. In the authors' perspective, reduction tactics disarm the opponents emotionally thereby facilitating more productive communication. Containment tactics include: 1) Fractionation—breaks down complex conflict situations into "smaller, more manageable units," 2) Negative Inquiry— seeks more information regarding criticisms and objections, 3) Metacommunication—shifts the focus of conflict from what is, to what could have been, or could be, 4) Response to All Levels of the Conflict—requests that opponents express completely the content and feelings about the issue, 5) The Position Paper—shares the absolute position on paper often communicates a desire for negotiation, 6) Compromise— attempts to give everyone something requested, 7) Establishment of Outside Criteria—asks the parties to agree to some form of criteria to help manage their conflict.[177] As one might expect, though the vocabulary is dissimilar, the approach parallels that of Leas but includes additional options and techniques.

---

[177] Gangel and Canine, 252-253.

The Reconciliation Model's Approach to Conflict
Containment. From the Reconciliation approach to conflict
management, Ron Susek offers procedural recommendations
following each of the five phases of conflict that
(metaphorically) follow the lifecycle of a firestorm. Many
serve to contain conflict. In phase 2, Sparks Igniting a
Firestorm, Susek makes these recommendations:

- Do not take a "wait-and-see" posture....
- Acknowledge there is a problem and call for fasting
  and prayer.
- Hold spiritual life meetings with a neutral visiting
  speaker....
- Exercise church discipline when it is appropriate....
- Invite a neutral mediator to help settle the
  disturbance....[178]

Following Phase 3, Firestorm in Full Fury, Susek
recommends:

- ...immediately seek a crisis management consultant.
- Prayerfully determine if there is an evil core to the
  firestorm and start church discipline.
- Keep a strong balance between grace and justice, both
  in preaching and dealing with people....

---

[178] Susek, 38.

- Consult with a Christian attorney to avoid an unnecessary lawsuit...
- Do not be indecisive about issues....[179]

To borrow Susek's metaphor; these conflict-containing strategies work as fire retardant or back-burning bringing greater control to the situation by slowing conflict's advance, or even halting it. This in turn gives managers more time to direct resources to the issue. There is also a biblical and spiritual demeanor to Susek's containment recommendations not overtly seen in Leas' and Gangel's lists, though there are structural and organizational similarities. By and large the literature does not deliberately seek to preclude either of these approaches to conflict management but there is a distinct difference in focus.

The Resolution of Church Conflict

"Resolution" is the term most often used in the literature to describe the end to which the intentional constructive processes of conflict management have been aimed. It is best understood as the process by which conflict's constituent parts are assessed. Differences can be eliminated or accepted but a decision is made to accept a solution that ends the hostilities. What the ending of

---

[179] Ibid., 47.

hostilities looks like is seldom addressed accept within the Reconciliation model. The introductory caution of Robert Wise is noteworthy. His *Leadership* magazine article, "When Mindsets Collide," argues that there are three problems with conflict resolution: 1) extremists can seldom every be satisfied, 2) one of the groups in conflict seems to lose more than the other, and 3) staff members are generally placed in a bind because they are rarely viewed as being impartial.[180] As these problems testify, conflict resolution seldom leads to pre-conflict conditions. Furthermore, as some of the literature would maintain, these three problems might indicate a "false peace"[181] or a "peacefaking"[182] that truncates the process prematurely.

The Managerial Approach to Conflict Resolution. Literature representing a more administrative managerial approach, best seen in the Speed Leas' tradition, establishes a clear process for conflict management. In its simplest form (collaborative), it includes 1) the institution of procedural guidelines that comprise a mutually-agreed upon timetable, agenda and rules for participation and behavior, 2) an

---

[180] Robert L. Wise, "When Mindsets Collide," *Leadership* 7:4 (Fall 1986): 27-28.

[181] Van Yperen, 169-175.

[182] Ken Sande, R. Schlaepfer, and J. Van Yperen, "Keeping Conflict Healthy," *Leadership* 25:4 (Fall 2004): 22.

acknowledgement, exploration and assessment of the problem(s) and its/their mutually-accepted definition, 3) the identification and clarification of the interests of the parties, 4) the gathering and sharing of data by all involved, 5) a mutual search for solutions to each problem with all alternatives accepted for evaluation, 6) the development of a clear, agreed upon decision-making process that leads to the selection of one solution by consensus for trial (negotiation, voting, arbitration or hierarchy if collaboration fails), 7) the opportunity for individuals indicted for misconduct (e.g. poor performance, inappropriate behavior) to respond personally to their accusers.[183] Each step includes its own strategies that are best implemented with the proper skills. In the Leas' model, higher levels of conflict require additional agreements up front devoted to reestablishing relationship and communication. This model's strength is that it offers people the hope of process, the security of structure, and the assurance of intentional but controlled confrontation.

A Biblically-Centered Approach to Conflict Resolution. Several authors have sought to outline the conflict resolution process by biblical principle alone. Horace Fenton's *When Christian's Clash* draws from the experience

---

[183] Leas, *Moving Your Church through Conflict*, 41-53.

of seven incidents of conflict amongst God's people recorded in the biblical story to develop guidelines restoring peace and unity to the Body. These principles, enumerated here, are interestingly similar to much of conflict management theory: 1) Take the initiative, 2) Use caution in making judgments, 3) Handle growing pains adequately, 4) Remember that we are on the same team, 5) Give both sides a fair hearing, 6) Heal the wounds of conflict, 7) Agree to disagree, 8) Confront out of obedience to the truth but in love, 9) Create a positive context for peacemaking.[184] Similarly, Leslie Flynn's book, *When the Saints Come Stormin' In*, develops principles of resolution from the incidents of conflict in the early church, mostly from the book of Acts. The reader is encouraged to 1) face the conflict, 2) acknowledge and listen to all sides, 3) be firm and courageous in his beliefs, and 4) exhort one another to view all factions as a complement to each other.[185] Another biblically-oriented book is *Surviving Church Conflict* authored by Dave Peters. Each of his chapters draws generously from the Pauline Epistles' instructions and the teaching of Jesus for peacemaking and reconciliation, building upon the themes of the 1) sufficiency of God's grace—His loving involvement in every situation, 2) primacy

---

[184] Fenton, 23-146.

[185] Leslie B. Flynn, *When the Saints Come Storming In* (Wheaton, IL: Victor Books, 1992).

of a life of worship—the believer's humble response to the cross demonstrated by his imitation of Christ, 3) Rule of Christ in Matthew 18—our obedience to the biblical methodology of peacemaking, allowing ourselves to be broken by the Spirit, and 4) ministry of peacemaking—an activity flowing from the believer's brokenness and experience of grace towards disobedience within the church and persecution from the world.[186] The common component within the writings of Fenton, Flynn, and Peters, as representatives of this approach, is their commitment to Scripture and the belief that within its precepts and examples lays God's wisdom in dealing with conflict. [187]

---

[186] Peters, 15-152.

The Redemption of
Church Conflict

The literature most frequently and substantially discusses conflict management in terms of its containment (reduction) or resolution as evidenced in the preceding sections. However, there is a portion of the literature that takes a radically different approach to church conflict, choosing to focus on redemptive elements such as reconciliation and restoration. This is not to say that that these concepts are not included in the bulk of church conflict management literature; it is plainly not developed there because the focus is placed on reaching secondary goals. Speed Leas, for example, sees the necessity of dividing the goals of conflict management into the ultimate and penultimate. He states that "The ultimate goal that we conflict managers might have ... obviously, is one of reconciliation where these groups move from estrangement to friendship, from enmity to amity."[188] Leas, however, considers it unlikely that the ultimate goal can be realized immediately, making it necessary to settle on attaining these five penultimate goals; 1) making clear decisions, 2) increase tolerance for difference, 3) reduce aggression, 4) reduce passive behavior,

---

[188] Leas, "The Basics of Conflict Management in Congregations," 35.

and 5) reduce covert manipulative behavior.[189] These five goals, and others he mentions elsewhere,[190] become the focus of the management process. The difference between these goals and Leas ultimate goal of reconciliation is notable.

It is that ultimate goal of reconciliation that has become the organizing idea for a number of writers and their works including, John Lederach's *The Journey Toward Reconciliation*, Ken Sande's *The Peacemaker*, Ron Susek's *Firestorm*, Dave Peters' *Surviving Church Conflict*, and Jim Van Yperen's *Making Peace*. What differentiates this literature is that, beyond the centralizing idea of reconciliation, there stands a biblically- based approach that looks almost exclusively to the Scriptures to explain and guide the entire conflict management process, including its purpose, means, model and methods.

The Biblical Purpose of Conflict Management

As bizarre as it might seem, one must look far and hard in the literature to find substantial discussion regarding conflict's "biblical" purpose. Frequently, the end in view has been captured by simple concept words such as "peace "resolution," "unity," or "reconciliation." Halverstadt states

---

[189] Ibid., 33-35.

[190] Leas, *Moving Your Church through Conflict*, 10-12.

that "God's peace provides the ultimate Christian vision for what makes a church fight Christian. The approximation of shalom is what an ethical process of management aims to realize. He recognizes, however, that "God's peace is a divine gift, not a human capability," and as such, it becomes "a transcending orientation toward which to steer...."[191] Like so much of the "resolution" material, Leas included, Halverstadt argues that the ultimate vision should be realized through "penultimate responsibilities of dealing with conflict situations":

- the vision of God's love of the parties and a process that requires respectfulness between parties;
- The requirements of God's justice for parties and a process that requires assertiveness between parties;
- The realization of God's truth among parties and a process that requires accountability between parties; and
- The healing of God's reconciliation for parties and a process that incorporates their differences within the framework of a larger good affecting all.[192]

---

[191] Halverstadt, 5.

[192] Ibid., 5-6.

Halverstadt's penultimate goals are laudable in their attempt to correlate to theological

themes such as love, justice, truth and reconciliation, but one wonders if the strategies can achieve that "transcending orientation" he describes as "shalom"— "God's peace."

Halverstadt and Leas' understanding of purpose establishes a useful backdrop from which to understand the literature that is written from the Reconciliation perspective which looks to broader theological themes to understand conflict's purpose. Van Yperen, for example, states that, "conflicts are God-purposed and always for our good."[193] Likewise, Ron Susek argues from the perspective of God's sovereignty in conflict (Isa 45:7), declaring that it is "allowed or caused by God" as part of the means of His predestinating.[194] So the real question is, one that must be central to any discussion pertaining to the purpose and goals of conflict management, "what is God's purpose for conflict?" Van Yperen contends that it is "to accomplish redemption. Every conflict is an opportunity to work out our salvation according to God's redemptive plan."[195] Following his discussion of biblical passages pertaining to conflict Les

---

[193] Van Yperen, 107.

[194] Susek, 116-117.

[195] Van Yperen, 107.

Moore surmises that the purpose of conflict is to glorify God, model servanthood and grow in the faith.[196]

This biblically-informed perspective on conflict's purpose has also been applied to conflict management. Susek suggests that every church adopt a statement of purpose for, 1) those involved in mediating the process: "Our purpose is to be God's instruments as he forms his Son more fully in each heart," and 2) the conflicted parties:

We will enact church discipline, not for punishment..., but for the purpose of:

- Repentance: to see the offender turn from wrongful behavior,
- Redemption: to bring the offender into a right relationship with God,
- Restitution: to bring justice where someone suffered wrong or loss,
- Restoration: to reestablish fellowship.[197]

These elements of repentance, redemption, restitution and restoration are most frequently encapsulated within the theme of reconciliation in this approach to conflict management. Van Yperen, who understands "making peace" and reconciliation as synonymous defines them as the

---

[196] Les E. Moore, "Interpersonal Conflict Resolution" (D. Min. diss., Biola University, 2003), 128-133.

[197] Susek, 128.

process of settling or resolving anything that separates and the restoration of that which has been lost—fellowship with God and His people.[198] Thus, reconciliation or peacemaking, is not merely an end but also a process—a conflict management process. John Paul Lederach, noting this connection, expands this concept even further in his understanding of reconciliation as a journey rather than a product of belief or a process. "It is a journey toward a place where Truth, Mercy, Justice and Peace meet."[199] Though appearing esoteric, the context upholds what writers from this model understand; that reconciliation is not so much a final state of being amongst people as it is participating in and cooperating with God's mission of bringing all things together towards a universal restoration in Christ (Col 1:20).[200] This is truly the Reconciliation model's genius; connecting God's and man's ministry of reconciliation together as the basis for conflict management within the cosmic context of God's universal mission. No greater purpose could be found, and no greater impetus could be given in seeking to deal with conflict.

---

[198] Van Yperen, 200.

[199] Lederach, 159.

[200] Ibid., 160.

The Biblical Means of Conflict Management

From a biblical perspective, the theme of reconciliation, as the resolution of conflict, is generally introduced in the literature against the backdrop of conflict's ultimate source—Satan and sin. Thus, reconciliation is seen by some as the central theme in Scripture and God's primary mission. "I view reconciliation as *the* mission, the organizing purpose around which we understand and see God's work in history."[201] Van Yperen agrees, but adds that Christ's work of reconciliation also forms the primary means of reconciliation—the church, within which and by which the believer is transformed. "...we live into our salvation by joining others in a specific way of hearing, seeing, thinking, acting, and being. The church becomes the place...where God's redemptive purposes take place."[202] God's purpose in the world is integrally connected to the way (means) in which He brings His mission to fruition.

What is not immediate obvious here, but worthy of development, is Van Yperen's close association between the reconciling work of Christ and that of His church. In his chapter, "Toward a Theology of Reconciliation," Van Yperen argues that the Gospel of Jesus Christ provides a salvation

---

[201] Ibid., 160.

[202] Van Yperen, 69.

that is past, present, and future as made plain by the doctrines of justification, sanctification, and glorification. The reconciling work of Christ in securing our justification demands transformation—the believer's sanctification. This work is carried out by the Spirit and the Word as the "corporate" act of submission and obedience. Van Yperen rightly understands that the ongoing work of reconciliation is found in the church where God's people are being transformed into Christ's image on the basis of His death ("cruciformed") and formed by His image through interaction in and with the Body of Christ.[203] From L. Gregory Jones' book, Van Yperen argues that the church is called to embody this ministry of reconciliation as the process (means) by which conflicted people are made whole:

> In the face of human sin and evil, God's love moves toward reconciliation by means of costly forgiveness. Human beings are called to become holy by embodying that forgiveness through specific habits and practices that seek to remember the past truthfully, to repair brokenness, to heal division, and to reconcile and renew relationships... (*Embodying Forgiveness: A Theological Analysis*, 49).[204]

Thus, Van Yperen posits two foundational principles to understanding the means of reconciliation: 1) Everything needed for reconciliation has already been provided in God's

---

[203] Ibid., 58-64.

[204] Ibid., 59.

Word, by His Spirit and through His Church, and 2) Reconciliation must always include all three: the Word, the Spirit, and the church.[205] Reconciliation as the means of conflict management assumes the context of genuine community (church fellowship) that has experienced forensic reconciliation.[206] The process of conflict management, then, requires unconditional submission to the authority of God's Word, His Spirit, and the church.[207] The question of how conflict is to be managed is framed against the backdrop of what God has already done— "reconciling the world to himself in Christ" (2 Cor 5:19).

The Biblical Model of Conflict Management

Lederach explains that God's redemptive work in Christ also demonstrates a model for reconciliation, a life of peace, justice and forgiveness that is to be incarnated in the lives of the believer and lived before the world.[208] What Lederach contends is that Jesus' incarnation as the very image of the invisible God (Col 1:15) was not only intended to accomplish reconciliation by His death on the cross, but demonstrate it as the way God deals with mankind out of His

---

[205] Ibid., 180.

[206] Ibid., 181-182.

[207] Ibid., 185-196.

[208] Lederach, 161.

love and grace. Additionally, Lederach argues that this way of reconciliation was modeled by Jesus on a day-to-day basis in His attitudes and the way He interacted with people. The Christian as a disciple of Christ is called to also incarnate His reconciliatory lifestyle by being an ambassador of peace, justice, and forgiveness both within and without the church.[209]

Van Yperen likewise understands reconciliation to be more "an embodied way of life" (1 John 1:5; 2:9-10) than "a collection of principles to be remembered or steps to be taken,"[210] It is a way of life to be lived into as one follows Jesus' example and submits to the power of the Spirit and His Word. Jesus' submission to the Father as the "humble, leadable, teachable" servant exemplifies the spiritual brokenness that is essential to the process of reconciliation, an example that is intended to be followed (1 Pet 2:21) as a way of living in reconciliation.[211] Dave Peters explains the relationship between reconciliation and brokenness: "Brokenness is a tool God uses in our lives first to correct ourselves before we can help others.... We engage in intensive introspection of who we are in relationship to Jesus

---

[209] Ibid., 162.

[210] Van Yperen, 180.

[211] Ibid., 188-192.

Christ and others."[212] Brokenness, then, is a means of preparing the conflict manager for a life and ministry of reconciliation.

In the same way that the purpose and means of church conflict management are informed by God's redemptive purposes and actions revealed in His ministry of reconciliation, the way in which conflict management processes are to be conducted is likewise informed. They are exemplified in the person and work of Christ and become the model for conflict management—one best described as being reconciliatory.

The Biblical Method of Conflict Management

In dealing with a genuinely biblical method of conflict management, something more than assessment, agreements and strategies is in view, though these may certainly be included. Literature from the Reconciliation model looks to employ strategies that conform to the biblical process of reconciliation. These have been made evident by way of example in God's redemptive work of reconciliation and in Jesus' reconciliatory lifestyle. Moreover, the literature recognizes that they have been canonized and institutionalized in Christ's injunction to the church found in Matthew 18.

---

[212] Peters, 84.

The "Rule of Christ" Establishes the Process for Redeeming Conflict

Profoundly, this text has been labeled, "the Rule of Christ" by the Anabaptists, a group whose long standing commitment to peacemaking is unrivaled.[213] As this passage indicates, conflict is anticipated in the church. This situation, however, must be met with confrontation that upholds 1) God's mission of reconciliation—to reconcile through Christ all things to Himself (Col 1:20), 2) His model of reconciliation—a humble, peacemaking servant, and 3) His means of reconciliation—forgiveness and restoration within the church. Matthew 18, then, is crucial to a theology of reconciliation. John Howard Yoder writes,

> It is the only place we find the word "church" reported as being used by Jesus himself. Its weight is accented by the account of Paul's asking the Christians in Corinth to use this procedure instead of going to the Gentile courts (1 Cor 6:1-8), and by the explicit command closing the letter of James (5:19-20).[214]

Jesus suggests three steps be taken in the reconciliation process, each one increasing the number of people involved and exposing the situation to greater public knowledge. Each

---

[213] Boers, 87.

[214] John Howard Yoder, *The Royal Priesthood* (Grand Rapids, MI: Eerdmans, 1994), 122.

step focuses on taking the initiative to confront the offense as well as to spend time "listening" to the offender. Yoder puts this passage in perspective:

> Matt. 18 is not recommended as guaranteeing the church's purity or reputation, exemplifying God's righteousness, making church membership demanding, or guarding against the erosion of values. The real purpose is reconciliation; i.e., the restoration of relationships. The priority of restoration is the reason for so many attempts. This procedure has been used as a tool for punishing people, but its evident hope is restoration and reconciliation.[215]

Yoder's understanding of the Rule of Christ agrees with what the literature conveys; the purpose of conflict management is reconciliation; involving self-examination, confession, repentance, forgiveness, restitution, and restoration. Each of these reflects an intensely spiritual dynamic that is part of the transformation process of all the parties involved.

These themes have been outlined by Van Yperen as part of the governing principles that underlie conflict management: Reconciliation, 1) entails self-examination in the context of community and assumes some culpability, 2) necessitates exposing sin (Eph 5:11), 3) requires practicing authentic communication—"speaking the truth in love" (Eph 4:15), 4) calls upon church leadership to take responsibility in lovingly confronting members who are in sin or exhibiting

---

[215] Ibid., 335-336.

difficult behavior by utilizing the biblical pattern (Matt 18), 5) encourages the open response of confession, the renunciation of sin as a way of life in the church (Jas 5:16), 6) calls for the church to grant forgiveness as a response of grace and love in Jesus' Name, 7) demands loving discipline and just restitution as the means of reconstituting character and completing restoration, 8) purposes to restore the sinner (Gal 6:1)—the reintroduction of the individual to the community for worship, fellowship, growth, and service.[216] It is the completion of this process that brings about the biblical condition of shalom—peace.[217]

Spiritual Confrontation Actuates the Process of Redeeming Conflict

A process to actuate these governing principles of reconciliation is found in much of the literature representative of this approach. Van Yperen suggests an eleven-step guideline for leading a confrontation meeting. This is his equivalent of the conflict resolution approach as represented by Speed Leas. However, the change in language, style, and content should be carefully noticed.

1. Pray. Thank God for what He is going to reveal and do....

---

[216] Van Yperen, 177-254.

[217] Halverstadt, 4.

2. Explain the goal of reconciliation. Explain how and why all are there: to seek reconciliation....
3. Accept the lordship of Jesus Christ. ...all are loved, respected, and valued....
4. Enter into the light. Define current reality by exposing sin and stating clearly, specifically, and objectively the exact nature of the conflict or problem....
5. Submit to God's truth... Introduce Scripture as a standard to follow....
6. Describe the nature of the problem and what proper obedience would be....
7. Discuss viewpoints. Invite response and discussion. Allow differing descriptions... Validate feelings and concerns... as clarifying questions....
8. Discern God's voice and will. Summarize the differences and agreements... Ask each party to consider what it would mean for him, personally to submit to the Holy Spirit and to each other "in the Lord"....
9. Decide to act. Ask each participant what he/she is prepared to do.
10. Commit to act. Inform and agree upon specific next steps for confession, reconciliation, and restitution.
11. Pray...Thank God for grace and forgiveness...through ...Christ.[218]

The end result—the goal—is peace, which is the fruit of God's Spirit formed in biblical community. "Making peace is the result of God's people being claimed by and putting into practice the Gospel story."[219] That "Gospel story" is the story

---

[218] Van Yperen, 217-220.

[219] Ibid., 256.

of God's ongoing work of reconciliation in the world through the church and expressed particularly in how His people are being mutually transformed.

Like other writers, Van Yperen readily admits that not all efforts at reconciliation end well which is why he states that "Reconciliation is a long walk no believer can make alone. It is living by faith in a disciplined community under God's Word and Spirit."[220] But it is this very point—the disciplined community—that is at the center of the reconciliation model. Reconciliation is a way of life, a culture within the community of faith that is "created" and "reinforced" deliberately and repeatedly by its leaders.[221]

---

[220] Ibid., 252.

[221] Sande, Schlaepfer, and Yperen, "Keeping Conflict Healthy," 27.

Summary

This Literature Review demonstrates that though the issue of church conflict is a relatively recent field of professional academic study, it has become the focus of increased concern because of the growing awareness of its debilitating effects on the church.

Research has shown that there is a natural relationship between the extent of conflict in the church and its vulnerabilities as a socio-political voluntary organization. Because of the extent of church conflict there is a need for its management, a situation made even more critical because of conflict's inevitability. These inevitabilities are necessarily normal; first, because of the nature of the church as a unique organization reflected in it theological, sociological, and psychological makeup; and second, because the Scriptures mandate peacemaking and call the church body to experience its unity.

Since the church is both vulnerable to conflict and predictably assured to experience it, the ability to diagnose it becomes the logical next step in managing it. This calls for a deeper "understanding" of conflict, particularly as it exists within the church. It is not enough to know that conflict exists; what is required is an understanding of what it is, where it comes from, and how it works. Attending to these issues facilitates conflict management which can be understood as a relatively complex, humanly-contrived system that seeks to intentionally use relational processes to resolve the problem(s) in question.

It is the primary intent of the literature to offer such systems, which we have called "approaches." Approaches vary, but as the literature indicates, all offer unique and constructive strategies for dealing with church conflict that can and should be utilized by the practitioner in an integrated way as the situation prescribes.

What must be gleaned ultimately is that conflict management, like reconciliation, is a way of life for the church and the normal state of conducting its affairs, be they substantive, interpersonal or intrapersonal. Life is conflict and conflict is to be lived in the context of reconciliation, a way of life that incarnates God's redemptive purpose in the world and embraces the reconciliatory lifestyle of Jesus.

The church has been both called and invited to experience peace and unity by confronting its sinfulness, engaging in mutual confession and forgiveness, utilizing this experience as part of reconciliation's purpose—to form God's community by transforming its members into Christ's likeness.

Bibliography

Armstrong, Leroy R., Jr. "When Not to Confront."
  Leadership 14:1 (Winter 1993): 73-74.

Barna, George. *A Fish out of Water*. Brentwood, TN:
  Integrity Publishers, 2002.

Bartel, Daniel J. "The Christian Homeschool Movement and
  the Traditional Church." D. Min. diss., Covenant
  Theological Seminary, 1998.

Boers, Paul. *Never Call Them Jerks*. Bethesda, MD: Alban
  Institute, 1999.

Bossart, Donald E. *Creative Conflict in Religious Education
  and Church Administration*. Birmingham, AL:
  Religious Education Press, 1980.

Burnham, Monty, W. Egmont, R. Hagstrom, G. MacDonald,
  and P. Toms. "Leadership Forum. Conflict: Facing It
  in Yourself and in Your Church." *Leadership* 1:2
  (Spring 1980): 23-36.

Bustanoby, Andre. "Wars You Can't Win." *Leadership* 14:1
  (Winter 1993): 56-63.

Buzzard, Lynn. "War and Peace in the Local Church."
  Leadership 4:3 (Summer 1983): 20-30.

Buzzard, Lynn R., and Laurence Eck. *Tell It to the Church*.
  Wheaton, IL: Tyndale House Publishers, 1985.

Clinton, Robert J. *The Making of a Leader*. Colorado
  Springs, CO: Nav Press, 1988.

Cosgrove, Charles H., and Dennis D. Hatfield. *Church Conflict: The Hidden Systems Behind the Fights*. Nashville, TN: Abingdon Press, 1994.

Dobson, Edward G., S. B. Leas, and M. Shelley. *Mastering Conflict and Controversy*. Portland, OR: Multnomah Press, 1992.

Dudley, Carl S., and Earle Hilgert. *The New Testament Tensions and the Contemporary Church*. Philadelphia, PA: Fortress Press, 1987.

Edwards, Gene, and Tom Brandon. *Preventing a Church Split*. Scarborough, ME: Christian Books, 1987.

Eitzen, D. Stanley, and Maxine Baca Zinn. *In Conflict and Order: Understanding Society*. 9th ed. Boston: Allyn and Bacon, 2001.

Engstrom, Ted W., and Edward R. Dayton. *The Christian Executive*. Waco, TX: Word Books, 1979.

Fenton, Horace L., Jr. *When Christians Clash*. Downers Grove, IL: InterVarsity Press, 1987.

Flynn, Leslie B. *When the Saints Come Storming In*. Wheaton, IL: Victor Books, 1992.

Friedman, Edwin H. *Generation to Generation: Family Process in Church and Synagogue*. New York, NY: The Guilford Press, 1985.

Galli, Mark. "Epilogue." In *Mastering Conflict and Controversy*, ed. Ed Dobson. Portland, OR: Multnomah Press, 1992.

Gangel, Kenneth O., and Samuel L. Canine. *Communication and Conflict Management in Churches and Christian Organizations*. Nashville, TN: Broadman Press, 1992.

Goetz, David L. "Forced Out." *Leadership* 17:1 (Winter 1996): 40-54.

Goodman, Denise W. *Congregational Fitness.* Bethesda, MD: Alban Institute, 2000.

Habecker, Eugene B. *The Other Side of Leadership.* Wheaton, IL: Victor Books, 1987.

Hall, Jay. *Conflict Management Survey.* Woodlands, TX: Teleometrics International, Inc., 1996.

Halverstadt, Hugh F. *Managing Church Conflict.* Louisville, KY: Westminster/John Knox Press, 1991.

Haugk, Kenneth C. *Antagonists in the Church.* Minneapolis, MN: Augsburg Publishing House, 1988.

Himes, J. S. *Conflict and Conflict Management.* Athens, GA: University of Georgia Press, 1980.

Huttenlocker, Keith. *Conflict and Caring: Preventing, Managing, and Resolving Conflict in the Church.* Grand Rapids, MI: Ministry Resources Library, 1988.

Hybels, An Interview with Bill. "Standing in the Crossfire." *Leadership* 14:1 (Winter 1993): 14-22.

Johnson, David, and Frank P. Johnson. *Joining Together: Group Theory and Group Skills.* Englewood Cliffs, NJ: Prentice Hall, 1975.

Kirkland, Robert W. "Conflict Management in the Church." *Search* 20:4 (Summer 1990): 12-15.

Kraybill, Ronald S. *Repairing the Breach.* Scottdale, PA: Herald Press, 1981.

_____. "Handling Holy Wars." *Leadership* 7:4 (Fall 1986): 30-38.

Kreider, Robert S., and Rachel Waltner Goossen. *When Good People Quarrel: Studies in Conflict Resolution.* Scottdale, PA: Herald Press, 1989.

Leas, Speed B. *Moving Your Church through Conflict.* Washington, D.C: Alban Institute, 1985.

_____. "The Basics of Conflict Management in Congregations." In *Conflict Management in Congregations,* ed. David B. Lott. Bethesda, MD: Alban Institute, 2001.

_____. "Inside Church Fights: An Interview with Speed Leas." *Leadership* 10:1 (Winter 1989): 12-20.

Leas, Speed B., and Paul Kittlaus. *Church Fights: Managing Conflict in the Local Church.* Philadelphia: Westminster Press, 1973.

Lederach, John Paul. *The Journey toward Reconciliation.* Scottdale, PA: Herald Press, 1999.

Lewis, G. Douglass. *Resolving Church Conflicts: A Case Study Approach for Local Congregations.* San Francisco: Harper and Row, 1981.

London, H. B., and Neil Wiseman. *Pastors at Risk.* Wheaton, IL: Victor Books, 1993.

Malony, H. Newton. *When Getting Along Seems Impossible.* Old Tappan, NJ: Fleming H. Revell Co., 1989.

_____. *Win-Win Relationships: 9 Strategies for Settling Personal Conflict without Waging War.* Nashville, TN: Broadman & Holman Publishers, 1995.

McSwain, Larry L., and William C. Treadwell, Jr. *Conflict Ministry in the Church*. Nashville, TN: Broadman Press, 1981.

Miller, John M. *The Contentious Community: Constructive Conflict in the Church*. Philadelphia: Westminster Press, 1978.

Moe, Kenneth Alan. *The Pastor's Survival Manual*. Bethesda, MD: Alban Institute, 1995.

Moe, Lyndel John. "A Comparison of Two Analytical Models for Understanding Local Church Conflict." D. Miss. diss., Biola University, 1999.

Moore, Les E. "Interpersonal Conflict Resolution." D. Min. diss., Biola University, 2003.

Palmer, Donald C. *Managing Conflict Creatively*. Pasadena, CA: William Carey Library, 1990.

Pappas, Anthony G. *Pastoral Stress*. Bethesda, MD: Alban Institute, 1995.

Peters, Dave. *Surviving Church Conflict*. Scottdale, PA: Herald Press, 1997.

Pneuman, Roy W. "Nine Common Sources of Conflict in Congregations." In *Conflict Management in Congregations*, ed. David B. Lott. Bethesda, MD: Alban Institute, 2001.

Prinzing, Fred W. *Handling Church Tensions Creatively*. Arlington Heights, IL: Harvest Publications, 1986.

Rainer, Thom S. *High Expectations*. Nashville, TN: Broadman & Holman Publishers, 1999.

Reed, Eric. "Leadership Surveys Church Conflict." *Leadership* 25:4 (Fall 2004): 25-26.

Rendle, Gil. "The Illusion of Congregational 'Happiness'." In *Conflict Management in Congregations*, ed. David B. Lott. Bethesda, MD: Alban Institute, 2001.

Rumford, Douglas J. "Cacophony or Symphony." *Leadership* 7:4 (Fall 1986): 96-100.

Sande, Ken. *The Peacemaker: A Biblical Guide to Resolving Personal Conflict*. 3rd ed. Grand Rapids, MI: Baker Books, 2004.

Sande, Ken, R. Schlaepfer, and J. Van Yperen. "Keeping Conflict Healthy." *Leadership* 25:4 (Fall 2004): 20-27.

Shawchuck, Norman. *How to Manage Conflict in the Church*. Irvine, CA: Spiritual Growth Resources, 1983.

Shawchuck, Norman, and Robert Moeller. "Animal Instincts." *Leadership* 14:1 (Winter 1993): 43-47.

Shelley, Marshall. *Well-Intentioned Dragons: Ministering to Problem People in the Church*. Waco, TX: Word Books, 1985.

Steinke, Peter. *How Your Church Family Works*. Bethesda, MD: Alban Institute, 1993.

_____. "Outbreak." *Leadership* 18:3 (Summer 1997): 46-49.

_____. "Top Ten Anxiety Triggers." *Leadership* 18:3 (Summer 1997): 48.

Steinke, Peter L. *Healthy Congregations: A Systems Approach*. Bethesda, MD: Alban Institute, 1996.

Susek, Ron. *Firestorm*. Grand Rapids, MI: Baker Books, 1999.

Thomas, Frank A. *Spiritual Maturity: Preserving Congregational Health and Balance*. Minneapolis, MN: Fortress Press, 2002.

Vale, John W., and Robert B. Hughes. *Getting Even: Handling Conflict So That Both Sides Win*. Grand Rapids, MI: Zondervan Publishing House, 1987.

Van Yperen, Jim. *Making Peace*. Chicago: Moody Press, 2002.

Wallace, John. *Control in Conflict*. Nashville, TN: Broadman Press, 1982.

Westerhoff, Caroline A. "Conflict: The Birthing of the New." In *Conflict Management in Congregations*, ed. David B. Lott. Bethesda, MD: Alban Institute, 2001.

Willimon, William H. *Preaching About Conflict in the Local Church*. Philadelphia: Westminster Press, 1987.

Wise, Robert L. "When Mindsets Collide." *Leadership* 7:4 (Fall 1986): 22-28.

Yoder, John Howard. *The Royal Priesthood*. Grand Rapids, MI: Eerdmans, 1994.

Made in the USA
San Bernardino, CA
16 September 2015